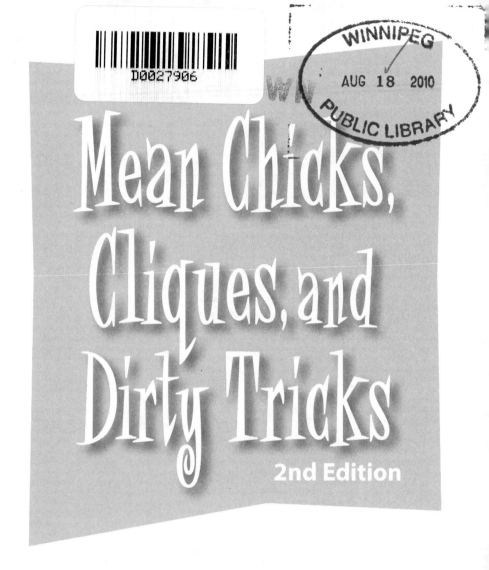

Mean Chicks, Cliques, and Dirty Tricks

2nd Edition

A Real Girl's Guide to Getting Through It All

Erika V. Shearin Karres, EdD

Aadamsmedia

Avon, Massachusetts

Published by
Adams Media, a division of F+W Media, Inc.
57 Littlefield Street, Avon, MA 02322. U.S.A.
www.adamsmedia.com

ISBN 10: 1-4405-0376-1
ISBN 13: 978-1-4405-0376-4
eISBN 10: 1-4405-0720-1
eISBN 13: 978-1-4405-0720-5

Printed in the United States of America.

10   9   8   7   6   5   4   3   2   1

Library of Congress Cataloging-in-Publication Data
is available from the publisher.

This publication is designed to provide accurate and authoritative information
with regard to the subject matter covered. It is sold with the understanding
that the publisher is not engaged in rendering legal, accounting, or other professional advice. If legal advice or other expert assistance is required, the ser-
vices of a competent professional person should be sought.

—From a *Declaration of Principles* jointly adopted by a Committee of the
American Bar Association and a Committee of Publishers and Associations

Many of the designations used by manufacturers and sellers to distinguish their
product are claimed as trademarks. Where those designations appear in this
book and Adams Media was aware of a trademark claim, the designations have
been printed with initial capital letters.

This book is available at quantity discounts for bulk purchases.
For information, please call 1-800-289-0963.

Dedication

This book is for Elizabeth S. Hounshell and Dr. Mary D. Shearin, my two extraordinary daughters, and for Andrew M. Karres, my devoted husband, with all my love and thanks.

Also for June Clark, my amazing literary agent.

And for Andrea Norville, my brilliant editor, and all her outstanding colleagues at Adams Media, especially Meredith O'Hayre, for her beautiful and touching revision and for shepherding this second edition through! Thank you so much for your caring and kind assistance!

Acknowledgments

A very special thanks to all the girls who participated in my research and to my thoughtful teen readers and experts, especially to Anna Crossett.

Many thanks to Jim Jackson, a master teacher who has instructed and inspired tens of thousands of students.

And to Bettina Grahek. What a powerful educator and school leader she is!

Contents

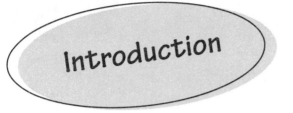

Introduction

More than any other time in history, it's a good time to be a girl. You have an incredible life ahead of you. You have so many choices, opportunities, and resources available to you. Things your mom, grandmother, and maybe even your older sister could only dream of are right at your fingertips. And now that you're a teenager, you're at the beginning of these most exciting times.

Yes, it's all starting to happen—the thrilling times you were looking forward to—like having a bunch more freedom, independence, and a later curfew. Your driver's license is right around the corner. You may be looking forward to moving on to middle or high school and all the cool extracurricular activities you love like soccer, drama, and school dances, maybe even a boyfriend.

Fashion wise, you're coming more and more into your own by defining your personal tastes and finding what you like and what you loathe.

But most of all, right now is when you start standing on your own two feet and relating to your friends in a closer way. Now the camaraderie of other girls really rules, and all of you can have tons of fun. Considering that almost everyone has cell phones, Facebook pages, and e-mail accounts, you can always be connected and constantly have your best buds only a click away. Yay!

Things are way different from when I grew up. But I always had one thing—the determination to make sure other girls didn't have it as rough as I did, that they wouldn't have anything or anyone get in their way! That's why I became a teacher, and later, what I am now—Dr. Erika, an advice giver who listens to and helps girls in particular.

In pursuit of this dream, I got the necessary education and job experience. Later, my own daughters grew up to become accomplished and productive adults. And what a joy it is, in return, to be able to pay back this great country by my work as an author and girl guru.

While writing the first edition of this book and now this super updated one, I polled more than 1,000 teen girls who attend various middle and high schools, from small to large and from all over, and asked them (or had their teachers ask them) the following: What, in your opinion, is a major problem for girls today?

The girls blurted out, "Other girls! They get in our way because they're so mean." Their teachers agreed, saying, "That's right. We see signs of girls acting aggressively on a daily basis."

So I went back to the girls and asked: Have you ever been a victim of girls being mean or been witness to it? And without exception, they all nodded, Yes! And they're even worse online. Some of the girls felt so strongly about the topic that they started peppering me with texts and e-mails, which you will see throughout the book.

NEW TEXT FROM BRIANNE, 15: I think every girl has been hurt in some way or made fun of by another girl or a group of girls once in their life.

 You have one new e-mail: Me & my friends have been cyber bullied constantly, and even on the phone. ~Kayla, 16

But when I asked the girls to give me some details on the behavior of their peers, all I got was silence. Their only response was to roll their eyes. Some of them just nervously looked down at their iPhones or BlackBerrys. It was clear that what had happened to them bothered them, and yet they had no clue how to fix the problem.

 NEW TEXT FROM DORY, 16: To ask a girl if she's ever been treated mean by another girl or girls [is] like asking if she's ever been around her peers.

Whoa! Looks like the subject of mean girls is pretty much taboo, even today! And the teachers' responses? These were even worse; they really clammed up. They swept the meanness and cyber bullying under the rug.

Yet, like the girls, they admitted that the treatment among girls is a huge problem in their schools. They even 'fessed up that a lot of girls could do way better in class if they didn't have to worry about other girls being mean to them.

Could it be that the teachers were afraid to have one more job on their plates? Or were they afraid they were in over their heads? Maybe they were being bullied, too, not in texting but with mean note writing and nasty things written in the boys bathroom, and they thought girls picking on girls was just a part of growing up, you know?

Whatever the teachers' reasons, a few girls were heroines by opening up to me. Sad personal stories poured in when I told them that I did not want to know:

★ Their names
★ The names of their schools
★ Their teachers' names
★ The names of their towns, cities, or states
★ Anything that could identify them, their parents and families, or their backgrounds in any way. Also, all the names of the girls who contributed are changed to protect them.

Girls furiously texted, posted, and e-mailed me really sad stories.

You have one new e-mail: Have you ever made fun of another girl? If your answer is no, more than likely you're lying your head off. If your answer is yes, you're not totally a bad person. You're just telling it like it is. ~Annie, 16

Soon, I had stacks of notes, texts, and e-mails about the ugly reality of girls hurting other girls, and how painful it is to be the butt of their cruel jokes or to be picked on for your looks. Even worse is when these mean messages are shared with everyone via Facebook, MySpace, and Twitter.

You have one new e-mail: I've been picked on about my hair all my life because I have curly and bushy hair. My best friends call my hair "nappy roots" and laugh. ~Natasha, 17

It's tough to be laughed at. Or pinched or kicked, for that matter! Having rumors spread about you not to just a few but all over school and beyond is certainly no fun. And while I could easily sense the pain of the victims, the victimizers clearly needed help, too, and ASAP!

So, now help is here! By reading this book, you show that you care and want to make the girl world a much better place. And you are going to succeed. I know it.

You're a heroine because you want to do what you can to help. Only, there's one problem: How can you spot the mean-girl types? And how can you get a handle on them now and in the years to come? More importantly, how can you help them? And how can you clean up cyberspace and disarm and deflate the bullies?

Most of all, how can you be sure not to let anyone or anything—not even the meanest texts and Facebook posts—get in your way? Read on.

Part I
Meet the Mean Girls

L et's face the facts: Even if you haven't met any mean girls in person yet, they exist in every school. So what can you do should they target you? A whole lot!

First, you can use your potential and power to learn all about them: about the way they act, what makes them tick, and what makes them turn to mean cliques. Then you can learn how to stop them in their tracks! Get them to clean up their bully behavior. At the very least, you can learn to refuse to let them affect you. You can learn to delete their misuse of technology, which is supposed to be used to keep in contact with friends, not for the bad of the girl world. You're an intelligent, empowered girl—the one who will run the show shortly if she doesn't already. There's no other girl in the whole wide world with your smarts, heart, and determination. You're the leader of the future and these are your years! So step up and don't let anything or anyone stop you on your quest to be the best.

The truth is, some girls can do some way mean things. They can be flat-out unkind, openly ignoring other girls, picking on them, or in extreme cases, actually hurting them physically or trying to crush their heart forever. If you haven't seen any of these girls, odds are you will witness some of this behavior shortly, either as a bystander or an unlucky target. But don't worry—you have the power to get on top of this situation and benefit from it. And as you learn about and conquer the new ways in which mean girls are mistreating other girls these days through blogs, Twitter, text messaging, Facebook, MySpace, and so on, you will learn new ways to change this behavior—or at least how you react to it. Yes, you will turn the meanness around, do your best to help the types of girls who resort to these activities, and avoid being victimized. And then you will blossom better and bigger than you might have if you didn't have the mean chicks to try their tricks.

You have one new e-mail: There's a purpose or lesson to be learned in every event that occurs in someone's life. You reap what you sow. Next time you decide to diss someone always remember, what goes around comes around. ~Jeni, 16

So, by the end of this book, you'll be able to spot whatever not-nice girl acts are out there in your school, community, and online. Fact is, some mean girl behavior isn't immediately obvious. It can be covered up with a syrupy smile or be disguised in some other way. Hey, some mean chicks' tricks might even look cute when observed from a distance. Some girls might pretend they're someone else online, acting like a cool guy, trying to catch you unawares. They think they've got you fooled, but you're not. 'Cause reading this book will open your eyes wide. Yeah, you will be able to spot them from a mile away, and you'll be able to deal with them in nothing flat.

No matter what people call the mean girls at your school—Snobs, Gossips, Traitors, and so forth—behind their backs, let's get one important thing absolutely straight first: When we discuss the kinds of mean girl behaviors that exist today, we are going to use these same terms, but only to save time. That is, rather than saying a girl has tendencies to act like a snob most of the time, we're just going to generalize and call her a Snob, and so on. But under *no* circumstances does that mean she will always be a snob or that we should forever condemn or demonize her; it's not the girl we're criticizing, only her way of acting or treating other girls. So, we might not like her actions or the way she expresses herself, but it *never* means we don't like the girl. Underneath, she has what all girls have—tons of potential and a terrific future ahead, especially if you point her in the right direction or show her a good example.

Chapter 1
The Snob

You see her cruising with her gal pals in her brand-new SUV, shopping at the most expensive stores, and getting away with murder at school. The slightest glance toward her in the halls can either make your day or ruin it, depending on her mood. Her hair is always perfect, her clothes just right. She dates the cutest guys and has all of the teachers wrapped around her little finger. She has the best parties and the coolest friends. You've just encountered the Snob.

DEAR DR. ERIKA:
There's this girl in my class who thinks whenever she opens her big mouth everybody better shut up and listen. And at lunch she sits at the best table in the cafeteria, and if you sit there, she pitches a fit. She actually gets her way in everything. Even the teachers are scared of her and treat her different from the rest of us.
~Reina, 14

DEAR DR. ERIKA:

I totally dread my second period class. There's this girl who, like, brags about everything. When she makes a good grade, she acts like she's the smartest. When she has a birthday party, she goes, "There's never been another party like mine." When she blabs about her family they're like sooo rich! And she cuts people and makes me feel like I'm dirt.

~Erica, 15

Sounds as if both Reina and Erica are dealing with the Snob, also known as a Spoiled Brat, Brag, and Name-Dropper.

FYI

No matter what type of show she may put on at school or with her friends, try to remember that the Snob is just a girl with problems, worries, hopes, and fears—just like you!

Sure, the Snob's issues may be different from yours. Most likely, for all of her cool clothes and popularity, deep down, she feels unhappy. She feels as if there's a big hole in her—like she's always trying to fill a void within herself. Maybe she was spoiled as a child and everything was done for her. Or maybe her parents got divorced and she was  ignored and now wants what she didn't get before—namely, attention. But the most likely scenario is that the Snob never got the one thing all little girls everywhere want—a steady stream of love and attention from her mom and or dad. What this girl got instead was material things, and plenty of them. Whoever raised the Snob may not have had time for her and tried to make up for it with oodles of doodads. So now, the Snob covers up her hollow part inside by overemphasizing *stuff.*

She gets her kicks out of shopping and mall crawling. What she adores are fancy designer shoes, Louis Vuitton bags, and serious jewelry. She may even see people as things—as expensive, classy items to enrich herself with, and in doing so, she also disregards their feelings. Of course, in the process, she doesn't necessarily mean to be rude, but comes across as arrogant and selfish and into herself all the time. She has to have her way all the time and acts like a baby when she doesn't. Her value system and her self-esteem are based on what valuables she has, so she carries on like a mini queen. In school, she's often the most popular girl in her grade even though—behind her back—many students call her a spoiled brat.

A close cousin to the Snob is the Name-Dropper. That's a girl who might not have been showered with tons of toys, but her family knows a fleet of "famous" (to one degree or another) people. So instead of getting her self-esteem from stuff, which the Snob, Brat, and Brag do, the Name-Dropper gets hers from dropping famous names. Oh, how she loves to mention the most popular guy in the senior class, the top athlete, or her cool neighbor. She seems to know them all or at least the inside scoop about them.

Instead of focusing on what they can do to better themselves, the Snob and her cousins focus on what they have and measure what others have (or don't have) against their own possessions.

But don't be fooled by her exterior; it's very possible that stripped of her fancy clothes or friends, the Snob has the same insecurities as everyone else. Even though she's carrying the latest Kate Spade bag or sporting the hottest new haircut while bragging about a text from a senior on her cheerleading squad as she prances down the halls with her entourage, maybe she's worried about the fight she overheard her parents having the night before or the history quiz in third period.

 NEW TEXT FROM CHAKA, 15: If you go around judging other girls as way beneath you all the time, you can't concentrate on what's most important—getting 2 B your personal best.

But rather than fess up, confide in a good friend, and discuss whatever's bugging her, the Snob wants other girls to feel miserable, too. This stems from her inability to face up to the fact that all isn't great in her life. So she dishes out plenty of cutting remarks in an attempt to make herself feel better.

 NEW TEXT FROM ANNYCE, 17: If UR making yourself feel better by ignoring other girls on purpose, U obviously have not been feeling great.

How true. The Snob and her close cousins never seem to feel that great. Why else would they act the way they do?

The fact is, by being mean to other girls, girls may get a rush of so-called superiority, but it's only temporary. Faux fine feeling at another girl's expense, in other words being okay with hurting another girl's feelings, is never good and is usually short lived.

 NEW TEXT FROM FLORA, 15: What U have to do is look at yourself first and see where you can improve b4 U criticize other girls and look down on them.

Having trouble believing that the Snob could ever have problems? Let's take a look at Tierney.

UNIVERSAL HIGH SCHOOL

Tierney attends Universal High School, but she doesn't get there the way most girls do—taking the bus, being dropped off by a parent, or riding with an older sibling. Most mornings, she zooms into the parking lot in her brand-new Beemer just before the tardy bell. She hops out of the car with her best girl pals in tow and dashes into school, where she deliberately slows down to a snail's pace, giggling and making plans for lunch.

There's no need to hurry—she knows if she slides into her seat by the last ring of the late bell, she won't be marked tardy. And even if she's not on time, no teacher would dare mark her down. Tierney has a way of coming up with more believable excuses than you can imagine.

And she delivers each one with such fake sincerity that you think, "Hmm, maybe it's true?" Plus, Tierney's parents are both big shots.

Should someone sit in Tierney's preferred seat—in the middle of the room, surrounded by all her friends—she just stands by the desk, rolls her eyes, and sighs until the unsuspecting student hops up in embarrassment and slinks into a corner of the room.

When the teacher assigns group work and puts a girl that Tierney doesn't associate with into her group, Tierney rolls her eyes some more (Nerd Alert!) until that girl hurriedly asks to trade places with one of Tierney's friends. Should the teacher protest, that "nobody" girl is frozen out during group work. No one will talk to her, like for forever.

Or maybe Tierney & Co. will say something nasty to the Nerd girl, making her do all the hard or dirty work on the group project—you know, take all the boring notes, do the annoying bibliography, cover the longest and most blah chapters, that type of thing . . . whatever Tierney and her gal pals don't want to do. In the meantime, they talk about what dresses they're going to wear to the prom, pulling out *Teen Vogue* and *Cosmo Girl* while the Nerd hops to it, beyond pleased to be allowed to do the grunt work.

When classes are over for the day, there's cheerleading practice. Tierney and her friends report to the gym, but again, in no hurry. Although most of her many friends are not on the squad, Tierney is, and she knows that practice won't start until she shows up; that's just the way it's always been. After practice, the girls all pile into her Beemer and grab a latte with skim milk at the Dairy Bar. Tierney drops her friends off at home one by one and then heads home herself.

As she pulls into the driveway, she can tell no one is home by the absence of cars. Yikes, for the first time all day, she's alone. Her girl buds will come over later, naturally, like they do every day if they know what's good for them. But for the moment the house is empty, which is the weirdest feeling. She almost hates to go inside, but she does.

Tierney kicks the front door shut, drops her books on a table, and heads upstairs. She flops onto her bed for a moment, thinking, "What do I do now?" She strides into her walk-in closet, jammed with the hottest clothes. Most things have been worn only once, if ever. In one corner sits a pile of shopping bags from brand-name stores that she hasn't unpacked yet. Great, something to do!

As she hangs up the new 7 jeans and Prada sweaters, she runs her hands over them, hoping to feel better. For a moment, she remembers how life used to be before her parents got divorced. They had time for her then. Mom wasn't gone all the time and Dad used to call her "his girl" and they would do fun stuff together. Now she sees him maybe twice a month. But hey, he just gave her another credit card with no limit, so that's something huge, right?

Tierney stops unpacking her latest purchases and calls her best friends. "Before pizza here, why don't we all meet at the Nordstrom makeup counter?" And tomorrow

Tierney will come to school in yet another super-great outfit, her friends surrounding her as they talk about what happened after they ate pizza, giving other girls a "you don't count" stare.

 NEW TEXT FROM MARIE, 15: But isn't the point of being popular to have friends? So why would you want to make enemies by acting like you're too good for other girls? It doesn't make any sense.

What you need to keep in mind is that underneath the Snob (or Snobs) is a girl who may not be so different from you—she may be a real nice girl just trying to emerge and surge ahead. Meanwhile, you still have to suffer from her actions. Or do you?

Take this quiz to find out if you can hold your own against the Snob.

FAST QUIZ

Snob Susceptibility—How Vulnerable Are You?

1. The Snob in your classes or among your group of friends has to have her way all the time. In order to deal with her, you:

   A. Stay as invisible as possible—it's better than getting on her bad side.

   B. Go along with her wishes, hoping she'll invite you to hang out with her sometime.

C. Speak out against her—and loud!—whenever you get the chance. You're not going to let her push you around!

D. Treat her the exact same way you would treat anyone else—she's no more special than the rest of your classmates.

2. You're in study hall reading *InStyle* when the Snob sashays over to you, asking in a sugary voice if she can "borrow" your algebra homework. She means COPY. You:

A. Make up a lame excuse to avoid helping her out—better to avoid her than to rock the boat.

B. Jump at the chance to do something for her, almost salivating inside—you never know where it will get you.

C. Give her your sweetest smile and give her your algebra homework from last week.

D. Tell her you don't let anyone copy your homework, but offer your help after school if she's having trouble.

3. You've been really pumped about auditioning for the lead in the school play, a musical. When you walk into the auditorium on the day of the tryouts, you realize the Snob is auditioning as well. You:

A. Sneak out of the auditorium as quietly as possible before anyone sees you. Why even bother? She always gets the lead anyway.

B. Rush up to her and tell her how totally perfect she is for the part. You're probably better off in the chorus, anyway.

C. March up to her and let her know she's got no claim on the part—and tell her she's tone deaf!

D. Step on stage and sing your heart out—better to give it your best than not to try at all.

4. You've been eyeing the most perfect pair of shoes for months and you finally have the money to buy them. You show up at school dressed to kill and ready to show off your new fancy footwear when you spot the Snob swishing down the hall in the very same shoes! You:

A. Haul your butt to the nearest bathroom, lock yourself in a stall, and don't come out until your girlfriends have scored you another pair of shoes—back to the drawing board!

B. Make sure you "just happen" to walk by her locker while she's standing there so she'll notice you have the same shoes. Compliment her on her taste and apologize profusely for having the same pair—they look better on her anyway.

C. Say, "Oh, look, we have the same shoes! How adorable! Wow, I never realized that your feet were SOOO BIG! It must be really hard for you to find your size!"

D. Don't make a big deal of it—you know you look great. With so many girls in one place, you're bound to have this dilemma once in a while.

Now it's time to find out how you did. How many As, Bs, Cs, and Ds do you have? Total up your answers then read on.

ANSWERS

If you answered mostly As: Okay, so we all know that the Snob can be intimidating even on her best days, but that's no reason to deny yourself happiness. You're allowing the Snob to have too much power over you and your decisions. Remember, seen in the light of day, even a firefly is just an ordinary insect. You have a right to be whoever you want to be. This is your time to shine—don't let the actions of others affect your powerful potential.

If you answered mostly Bs: Whoa, girl! You've got to give yourself a bit of a reality check. You are sooo at the mercy of the Snob! You've got to quit it, from this moment on. You can't live your whole life trying to please someone else, or soon you'll find you have nothing left that pleases you. You don't have to dance to her tune or give in to her whims anymore. Do you think your popularity will suffer if you stand up for what you want to do? When you let the Snob get away with her behavior, you're an enabler. Don't be one. Take a stand; be yourself. You may be amazed at what happens.

If you answered mostly Cs: Good for you! You make sure to speak your mind and not let the Snob take advantage of you. However, winning through disrespect to someone else may not be your best bet. You stand up to her, but at what cost? You've got a life and lots of great stuff to do—why add to your busy schedule by starting a war with the Snob? Keep up your strong attitude, but be ready to face the consequences of your not-so-nice actions! In the end, there's often a blowback from dissing somebody, even though they might deserve it.

If you answered mostly Ds: You go, girl! Pat yourself on the back—you've got it all together. You're an independent-minded girl who can recognize the Snob from a mile away. No way you'll ever let her get you down. You know your limits, and your long-term goals, and you handle yourself like a pro—calm, cool, and collected, that's your motto!

If you have a mixture of As, Bs, Cs, and Ds: Review all of the above. Obviously, there's a little bit of everything in you, which is great. Now, can you work on having a little less of the A attitude and a little more of the D?

No matter how you handle the Snob in your pack, know there's always at least one in any bunch of girls. So what should you keep an eye out for?

Snob Smarts: What Should You Know about the Snob?

★ Understand that the Snob has a problem that has nothing to do with you. Deep inside, she is insecure. She wants to cover up her insecurity and make herself feel better at your expense.

★ While it's so common for girls to feel this way, try not to be fooled. Just know that the problem belongs to the Snob, not to you. Condemn her behavior, not her.

★ The Snob might really need one true friend. Only if you feel like it, try to become the Snob's friend. Make a list of what is positive about her and see where you go from there. You might be amazed at how extending the hand of friendship can turn another person around.

 NEW TEXT FROM MANDEE, 15: I always felt like I was not good enough for any of them. That's the way the other girls were treating me, but that was wrong.

Correct, so next time you feel less than great in the face of the Snob, just think about the fact that maybe she isn't feeling so terrific on the inside. But you are and you have a plan. Move ahead. Until you have decided how you really feel about the Snob, what you need is a quick solution.

RAPID RESPONSE: WHAT YOU SHOULD DO ABOUT THE SNOB

There are number of things you can do to disarm the Snob and take away some of her power over you. Here are three to consider:

1. Be tough as you go through your school day. Draw on your inner strength and know you're as good as everybody else. There's no need to avoid the Snob—ever—unless it's because you don't have time for her foolish games.

2. Be as helpful as you can, if the Snob wants your help. However, be friendly but firm. Don't turn her down just because she's the Snob! Just make sure she's not taking advantage of your nice-girl nature. Don't let another girl use you.

3. Be prepared. Have a few kind but disarming stares or statements ready for whatever "superior" lines the Snob might lob your way. Practice these statements: "I'm glad you're doing so well" (when the Snob brags about her fabulous possessions); or, "Sorry you're having a bad day" (when the Snob disses you or your friends by flouncing away from you, with her nose held high); or, "The main thing is, you like them" (when the Snob drops the names of her A-list friends). Meanwhile, practice being modest and friendly to everyone. We teach and reach others best by example.

When I was in the eighth grade, we moved to another state and I had to go to school with a bunch of girls who were from a real nice neighborhood. And man, they never let me forget it. There was this one girl in particular. She would constantly gush about her perfect pool parties, her cabana that was way bigger than a house, and how much fun they had cooking out on their humongous patio. This kind of talk went on year round.

Needless to say, all the other girls got invited, but not me. This went on for two years. Then my dad got a big promotion and we bought a place at the lake. Dad said I could invite anybody I wanted anytime, but I waited for the right moment. Finally, when we were juniors, I volunteered to head up the prom committee, which was a big deal. We had to make the most important decisions about the theme, the color scheme, the music, the food, the caterer, and stuff. We had to pick out the photographers, videographers, order the invitations, get stuff mailed and approved, come up with the rules—I mean we had the power to decide every sweet detail that mattered. Wow. There were twelve of us, and I made sure I asked them all to the lake for an epic planning session, plus the advisors, too. But I made double-triple sure the invitation to Ms. Cabana got "lost."

Dr. Erika's Response

Good for you, Shoshanna, for taking the initiative to do something cool for yourself and your school. You stood tall in the face of the Snob and made smart decisions for yourself. But then when the tide had turned and you were in a position to show how much of a leader you had become, how you had really grown, you wimped out at a critical moment. You had such a great chance to set the record straight!

You should have taken this opportunity to clear the air, to invite or evite Ms. Cabana, but with a note attached. You could have said something like: *For two years you have not invited me to any of your pool parties, but that was your choice. My choice is to have you come to our lake house so we can all work on the prom preps together. You may feel awkward about accepting my invitation, but please do try to come . . .*

Something like that would have taught her a lesson. More importantly, it would have helped you move ahead. Revenge is a nasty motive; it's sneaky and pointless and it can be cruel. By mimicking Ms. Cabana's snotty actions, you enable her to keep acting like a snot. You'd better watch yourself in the future or you could end up turning into a Ms. Cabana yourself.

DEAR DIARY

Now that you've nailed down your snob susceptibility, you probably have a pretty clear picture of where you stand. In the presence of the Snob, do you turn into a meek little lamb? Or do you tell her what the real score is? No matter what your answer, chances are that there has been a time when someone said something totally rude to you or about you—as if you didn't count!—and that hurt your feelings. If that ever happened, it's time to get it off your chest—now.

Get out an old notebook; you know, the one that's almost empty from your least favorite class. Then, recycle that ratty-looking leftover notebook as your personal journal. Or you can start a new live journal online, but only for yourself. Whenever you read something in this book that sparks an idea or thought, jot it down. You may be surprised at how much better it makes you feel and how much you can learn about yourself! Throughout this book, there will be several journal exercises for you. Have fun with them, and don't be afraid to express your feelings. Here's a little exercise to get you started:

Are you totally bothered by the Snob in your class or your group of friends? Are there things she says or does that make you feel bad about yourself? We've all felt bad about ourselves at one time or another; it's just an unpleasant fact of life that we have to deal with—kind of like having a bad hair day or a pop quiz in history. Now, make a list of five things that make you feel bad about yourself in the face of the Snob. They can be anything at all—something she said to you or thoughts or feelings you have—don't hold back. After you've made your list, jot down or type up a few sentences (or pages, if you wish) that explain how these things make you feel. It's okay to get a tad mad, sad, or whatever—this is for your eyes only.

Now, let's take those negative feelings and turn them around! Next to each of the negative items, write five things that you love about yourself. Jot down a few sentences (or pages) about the things that make you feel good about yourself. It's okay to celebrate yourself every once in a while. In fact, it's a great reminder of the good things in your life. You're affirming and validating yourself—and that's awesome!

Finally, examine your lists closely and compare them. The next time you're around the Snob or faced with any situation that makes you feel bad, think of the good things from your list, and remind yourself that you and only you have the power to create your own happiness. Reread your list and smile wide. Congratulations! You've just made an attitude adjustment.

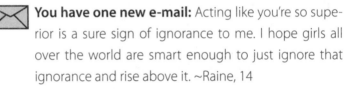 **You have one new e-mail:** Acting like you're so superior is a sure sign of ignorance to me. I hope girls all over the world are smart enough to just ignore that ignorance and rise above it. ~Raine, 14

FAB FIXES FOR WHATEVER ATTITUDE AILS YOU

You probably know how to accessorize an outfit—one day a chunky bangle, the next day a bunch of long necklaces, sometimes even a baseball hat.

Well, it's the same with attitudes. Many days you have a great attitude, even the best, don't you? But there are times when you feel like the entire world is out to get you. You've got these mood swings that can send you from Suzy Sunshine to Lindsay Lohan in thirty seconds flat. So who knows, you might slam doors, shrug, and not respond when your mom asks you something. You may clomp around the house, mumble, and mutter under your breath, or maybe you act like a snob yourself. Suddenly, you're feeling sooo superior to your friends or siblings.

This never lasts long, but it does happen. So what to do when you have a case of brattitude?

Check out some of these tips to improve your 'tude, no matter what kind of day you're having.

Rx: Battling Brattitude

Three times a day:

1. Look in the mirror and laugh at yourself. Really laugh out loud—we're talking belly laugh here. *If you don't feel it, fake it.* Then go back to looking at your prelaughing face. Do you really like that snobby, pouty, or bratty expression on your face? You know that the way we frown gets etched into our faces, don't you? Wouldn't you rather have happy laugh lines than bitter, sour-lemon ones as you get older?

2. Say you're sorry to all those people you were snobby or snooty to, and mean it, but if you don't, maybe you could fake it until you feel it, okay? Try it, starting today.

3. Do something nice for somebody else. This is a sure fix to getting your attitude back on track. Write a letter to a friend, clean the oven for your mom, and take your little brother to see the latest Disney cartoon movie. Okay, so it might not be as fun as the newest Zac Efron flick, but it's sure to be a good time.

It's amazing how making someone else smile can improve your disposition radically. Chances are, you'll end up smiling yourself and losing that brattitude ASAP. Remember, it's okay to have a bad day now and then, but acting like a clone of the Snob or allowing her behavior to influence your attitude is definitely not cool. By letting yourself shine, you'll encourage others to shine, too!

THE BOTTOM LINE

You know, though some girls in school shine and attract lots of attention and even get special privileges from some of their teachers, they might be nothing but fireflies. What does that mean? Well, seen in twilight, a firefly may appear to shine brightly; however, seen in bright daylight, that firefly is nothing more than a little insect—that's got everyone fooled but you.

 NEW TEXT FROM LIANNE CHO, 13: Some girls are so insecure they even bare their insecurity on the 'net. I mean really *bare,* know what I mean? I just wish they would grow up, c'mon.

So, try not to be taken in by the surface appearance of any girl in your school. Instead, try to look beneath the outer appearance. Get a feel for what's going on with girls like Tierney. Close your eyes to the way the Tierneys among us act and wait until their popularity wanes— which it will sooner or later (trust me!)—or until someone even more popular comes along, disses, and outdistances them.

But by checking in with yourself and with the girl teen scene at your school, you will be able to affirm what's good, abolish what's bad, and improve things overall. So know that you can do it: Deal with the Snob or her close cousins at your school or in your group of friends. Remember that she's someone who may be in pain and that her attitude and actions only affect you if you let them. Don't worry too much about her; instead, focus on the incredible choices you have all around you now and those that are waiting for you in the future.

> ✉ **You have one new e-mail:** No matter what you do, some girls will always think you're less than they are and not worth anything just 'cause they have an iPhone and you don't. What that really means is that they are immature and have a long way to go. ~Kristi, 17

Should you ever find any Snob/Brat feelings in yourself, suppress them or swat them away. Feeling superior to other girls because you have a bigger allowance or live in a nicer home or because your 'rents make way more money is very uncool.

Remember, you're never alone; you have your friends. And now, you have this book and your journal to help you through those tough moments. Think of them like you think of your favorite pair of sweatpants or jeans—

so comfy and familiar—knowing they'll always be there when you need them. Simply think of dealing with a Snob or Spoiled Brat as a little bump in the road—something that's got to be watched out for or stepped over and then put behind you just like that . . . with the snap of your fingers.

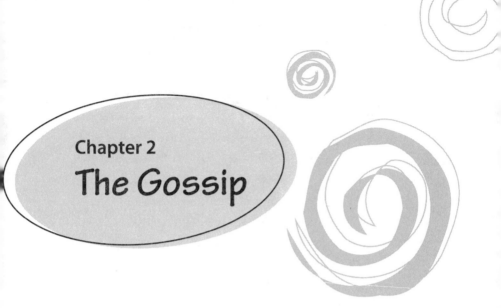

Chapter 2
The Gossip

She's always up on the latest gossip—who's dating whom, who got suspended, who's almost dating a college freshman—whatever it is, she knows it! Sure, she's super sweet to your face when she wants the scoop, but once she gets it, watch out! This girl can be a handful and a half. She spied, over your shoulder, on a text you wrote in algebra class and now it's all over the school. She saw you talking to your best friend's boyfriend and now she e-mails everyone that you're a man stealer! She's sweet sometimes, she's conversational often, and she's sassy nonstop. You've just encountered the Gossip.

DEAR DR. ERIKA:

More than anything, I hate when people are two-faced. There's this girl on my bus who acts so goody-goody. She starts talking to me and saying nice things. Then I hear from another friend what she says about me behind my back and the way she, like, runs me in the ground and calls me names and stuff. And before I know it, the fact that I stumbled gets twisted into me being "drunk." By lunch, everybody is talking about it. That afternoon, girls I don't even know whisper mean things about me. But whenever I confront the girl who started the rumor, she denies everything and acts so innocent, it kills me.

~Dee Dee, 15

DEAR DR. ERIKA:

I am so upset I don't know what to do. For years and years I was kinda big. So I asked the guidance department at my school to help me. They sent me to the cafeteria manager. She's a cool lady who gave me a bunch of pamphlets about nutrition and exercise. I read them from cover to cover. Then spring break came and I thought: Aah! What a perfect time.

So while my friends went off to the beach I said I wasn't feeling well and stayed home and started fixing myself some low-cal stuff to eat. You know, a toasted bagel with low-fat cream cheese for breakfast, salad for lunch, tuna and veggies for dinner. Stuff like that. And for sure, no more junk food. I dropped a couple of pounds during the first two weeks and ever since I've been losing more weight. Nothing drastic . . . slow and steady just like those books tell you to. And now everyone at school's saying I have anorexia! Even though I owned up about the dieting, now my "best" friend is spreading rumors about what I eat or not.

~Snow, 14

FYI

The Gossip, and her cousin, the Backstabber, are busybodies carrying around every tidbit of news like their precious iPods. The Gossip is always dishing the latest scoop, and does she have lots to talk about. Most of what she has to say is negative and is never about her. Instead, the Gossip picks up a tiny tasty tidbit of news and then she's off, flitting from friend to friend like a busy bee going from flower to flower, embellishing hugely on whatever she's just heard.

The bummer about the Gossip is that she could be a really good friend—she's tons of fun to talk to and she's a great communicator. But beware of the charms of the Gossip. Though it may seem like she's listening to your latest boy troubles with a sympathetic ear, when you share with the Gossip, you may find that your problems spread through the entire school and beyond 'cause she likes to post nasty Facebook comments on people's pages. Instead of using her telling talents for a good cause, like writing for the school newspaper, she uses her skills for no good at all.

You see, the problem with the Gossip is that she desperately wants to be admired and to feel like she's on top while you're not. Gossiping, in person or online, is the only way she knows to do that.

 NEW TEXT FROM BRYNNE, 13: How do you feel when someone gossips about you? Do you feel down? Low? Does it "mess" with your self-esteem? Sure it does, trust me.

The Gossip is self-aggrandizing and doesn't care whom she hurts. She's trying to make herself feel and look important by being in the know and spreading juicy chatter around the school. She's trying to build herself up with importance while bringing other girls down.

Imagine how much the Gossip could accomplish if she focused her time and energy on personal achievements rather than stepping on the backs of some girls who either don't know they're being gossiped about or are too polite or shy to speak up.

✉ **You have one new e-mail:** To be gossiped about is a gut-wrenching feeling. That's why I love to do it—my amusement at some other girl's expense. The feeling is all-mighty. But afterward I sometimes feel bad. ~Lindsey, 17

So, while the Gossip can be dangerous, don't write her off just yet. Gossiping, as I'm sure you know, is very fun.

You have one new e-mail: You feel powerful and popular by amusing other girls with your stories (well, lies or exaggerations)—also called hyperbole, according to my English teacher—about other girls. However, it's way different when the joke is on you. ~Abby, 17

Oftentimes the Gossip is just a teenage girl who needs an outlet for her talents so she won't turn on innocent classmates. She's really a creative people person, perhaps just a little misguided.

Maybe she only wanted dirt on you up until now because she wants attention. Try having a conversation about her—ask about her interests—and see if she brightens at the opportunity to chat about something other than gossip.

THE BACKSTABBER

A close cousin of the Gossip is the Backstabber. Whereas the Gossip is more of a secretive town crier, the Backstabber has two sides like a double-sided mirror. On side A, she ingratiates herself to you, acting all sweet until you confide in her. Then she takes that bit of info that you told her confidentially, embellishes it, and passes it on to anyone willing to listen.

 You have one new e-mail: Backstabbing is about the worst you can do. It makes the girl who's stabbed in the back feel like she can't ever trust anybody again. It could affect her for her whole life! ~Suzanne, 15

On side B, she joins the crowd of listeners and actually makes fun of the exact same girl she was formerly so nice to. So she betrays your trust, plus she often ends up being one of the worst offenders. Maybe she thinks whatever she's doing is just good-natured kidding about someone who's not present, but it goes far beyond that.

UNIVERSAL HIGH SCHOOL

With her glistening black hair, beautiful bright, dark-brown eyes, and ever-ready smile, Nikki is one of the most popular kids at Universal High. Walking into the guidance department, she smiles sweetly at the secretary and asks her, "Do you have a catalog from Berkeley?"

The secretary smiles back, "No, not at the moment, but I can request one."

"Would you please?" Nikki asks, "It's urgent!"

The backstory is that just last night Nikki examined herself critically again, so pleased with the way she looks. But why can't she grow more?

At five foot six, she's way too short to become a runway model, which is what she wants in a most major way. Correction: It's what she wanted; but no more. Since it doesn't seem like she's ever going to be over six feet tall, she's now thinking of going into business and opening up a modeling school. Does the University of Berkeley even have a business program for this, she wonders.

After leaving the guidance department, Nikki dashes to the cultural arts wing to meet the dance teacher who told

Nikki she would teach her how to walk properly. Of course, by then the bell has rung, but Nikki still has a pass from her homeroom teacher, so she's okay. "The office was, like, sooo busy" will be her excuse, and Nikki rehearses it as she stops in the restroom. Here, she uses the fingers of one hand to count up all the juicy tidbits she overheard this morning. There was that thing about the senior class president going home with the swine flu, the dish on the fight in the hall just before homeroom—all about something somebody posted on Facebook—and the class ring order date being set for next week. Now for the real interesting stuff: The captain of the football team was being chewed out in the principal's office about risking academic probation, and the candidate for homecoming queen was being tracked by her own mom. Nikki overheard the secretary reading the message aloud to the vice principal: "Just checking that my daughter made it to first period today. . . ."

But Nikki knows that she didn't. She saw Little Miss Homecoming with her own eyes totally skipping first period and reading People.com in the library. Oh, so much to tell her friends, so much to fill everybody in on!

Nikki pauses and smiles to herself. She's going over all the bits of gossip she's picked up so far and will gladly spread, but why? Because it makes her so powerful and so charming, admired, adorable—and so much in charge. Girls and guys, no matter what their cliques, want to talk to her to get the latest scoop. She loves being the center of attention, smiling through the hallway, feeling all of those eyes on her. Unlike what happens to her at home, where there is always an atmosphere of rush, rush, rush, gloom, and doom. Her parents are hard workers, but recently their store rent was increased, so they had to move their business into their home. Now both Mom and Dad work furiously, but it doesn't seem to make a difference—the economy is in the toilet and they're struggling. Worst of all, nobody gives Nikki any attention! She's invisible at home. At school, though, Nikki can push aside that stab of worry or wave of sadness. She has to be on all the time, and likes to make her friends laugh as she shares the school news.

Finally, she makes her way back to where she's supposed to be—World History class. The teacher checks her watch and frowns as she accepts Nikki's pass. Nikki joins her friends to do some group work. Before she can dish, however, a student whispers to her, "Did you know that the passes from the office now have a time stamp? If you're more than five minutes late, you're in big trouble."

OMG. Looks like Nikki just got caught, but punishment alone isn't going to help her. Someone needs to take time to clue her in that laughing at people and gossiping behind their backs is just as bad as actually saying something way mean to someone's face.

Way mean is right. As if you don't have enough stress in your life already without having to worry about dealing with gossip and backstabbing! Every girl has gossiped or has been the victim of gossip at some time in her life; no one is totally innocent here. Just remember that gossiping is cowardly behavior that has no good outcome. The

Gossip is seeking power, but you don't have to provide her with ammo!

Even if the victim tries to shrug it off, the Gossip and her buds can do some serious damage.

The Gossip is a smart cookie and she can sometimes be harder to spot than the Snob or the Teaser (discussed later). But her weapon is just as powerful, if not more so. Again, while her intentions may be misguided, try to remember that the Gossip has feelings just like you do and that intentionally hurting others is never cool. So, you can feel sorry for the Gossip, but first you should learn to protect yourself from her so she can't get in your way!

 You have one new e-mail: It's one thing to pick on someone behind her back, but it's another thing to say it to her face. I've had times where some girl will say something about me behind my back, but she doesn't have what it takes to say it to my face. But I don't worry about girls like her. They're just garbage to me. If I have something to say to someone, I say it to her face. ~Barbie, 16

Check out the quiz on the following page to find out if you're a target of the Gossip.

Gossip Go-Around—Don't Let It Happen to You!

1. You've just been through a really heinous breakup with your longtime honey and you're feeling pretty low. During first period, you take a bathroom break to clear your head. As you're washing your hands, the Gossip bounces through the door, notices you, and immediately begins to spout pseudo sympathy in order to get the scoop. You:

   A. Hesitate for a moment then tell her everything. You're terrified that if you don't, she'll just make up lies about you and then you'll feel even worse.

   B. Spill the beans immediately, basking in the glory of her attention for the moment, and hoping you'll be able to wrangle an invite to sit with her crew at lunch. Attention is attention, no matter where it comes from or in what form.

   C. Tell it all—and then some! The Gossip is like a walking tabloid and there is no such thing as bad publicity. Besides, spreading a little dirt around about your ex is the perfect revenge.

   D. Thank her for her concern, but tell her you'd rather keep it to yourself—your business is your business, and if you wanted the whole school to know, you'd post something on your Facebook page.

2. You're at the salad bar at lunch, wishing you had taken your mom up on her offer for that PB&J, when the

Gossip and a gaggle of her friends approach the bar whispering and giggling. She asks you if you've heard the latest dirt on Melanie, a quiet girl you sometimes talk to in study hall. You:

A. Listen and giggle along about Melanie's misery, even though you really don't want to. If you don't indulge the Gossip and her crew, you could be the next target.

B. Let them go ahead of you in line and anxiously join in the conversation—better to be part of the group than left out in the cold.

C. Dish, dish, dish! You eat up their gossip like it's today's lunch special and then share some down and dirty details of your own—nothing like a juicy rumor to spice up the school day!

D. Tell them thanks, but no thanks. If you have any desire to know what's going on in Melanie's life, you'll ask her yourself.

3. You haven't even made it to your locker Monday morning when you realize that you're the latest target of the Gossip. You:

A. Stay as invisible as possible for the next few days— the Gossip and her group will find another victim soon enough.

B. Laugh along with them and try to make a joke of it—hey, gossip happens to everyone and you don't want people to think you're a bad sport.

C. Become a one woman *Star Magazine*—no way you're letting the Gossip ruin your rep without ruining hers right back. Never underestimating the power of the written word, you launch an e-mail, Facebook, and Twitter campaign to keep the rumor going.

D. Hold your head high. You're as cool as a cucumber and walk the hallways as you normally do. "No comment," you say to the Gossip and her group when they inquire about the buzz. Your life is your business and you're not interested in petty school politics.

4. The Gossip has started a rumor about a close friend of yours that you know is a total lie, and the whole school is buzzing with the news. When people ask you about it, you:

A. Don't say anything about it. You'd rather not get involved in such a mess, and your friend can take care of herself.

B. Feel a little guilty, but tell every last detail you know. You'd hate people to think you're choosing sides.

C. Tell them every juicy detail you know and then throw in a few more over-the-top tidbits or bytes—if gossip is a crime, then you're public enemy number 1!

D. Tell them to get out of your face and leave your friend alone—don't they have anything better to do with their time?

Now it's time to find out how you did. Total up your answers.

ANSWERS

If you answered mostly As: What's the deal here? You're so afraid to speak your mind that you're letting others walk all over you. Would saying what you think or feel really hurt that much? What are you so afraid of? You're giving way too much power to the Gossip when you should be giving that power to yourself. You should give it a try sometime, you'd be surprised at how good you'll feel opening up and saying what's on your mind. You'll gain the respect of your friends and your peers and, most importantly, yourself.

If you answered mostly Bs: You're so starved for attention from the Gossip and her gang that you'll do anything it takes to win their approval—even if it means mimicking the Gossip's bad behavior. If you aren't loyal to your friends when they need you, who is going to be left to be loyal to you? In the future, when you are presented with any of these situations, try turning over a new leaf by being loyal to your friends and yourself. You may find that you enjoy the power of standing on your own rather than running with the pack.

If you answered mostly Cs: Okay, so if gossiping were a class, you'd have a 4.0. But it's not! You got off track here. You're in school to learn and become the best you can be and not to jibber-jabber about everybody's business but your own. You may be the best snooper-outer and dirt-digger in your school, but what good do those traits do you?

If you answered mostly Ds: The dish stops with you—good for you. You neither indulge in it nor listen to it. Hey, you like facts, not figments, so everyone knows they can come to you for the truth and nothing but the truth. There's nothing more powerful than being able to stop the Gossip at her own game and leave her squirming in the dust. A definite top score for you!

If you have a mixture of As, Bs, Cs, and Ds: Review all of the above. Obviously, there's a little bit of everything in you, which is great. Now, can you work on having a little more of that Answer-D attitude?

GOSSIP SMARTS: WHAT SHOULD YOU KNOW ABOUT THE GOSSIP?

However you get a grip on the Gossip, know that there's usually one or more in any group of girls. So how do you get those gossip smarts? Try the following:

★ Keep in mind that the Gossip is starved for attention. When she grew up, she probably didn't get enough at home and maybe she still doesn't. Sure, she may attract lots of attention at school, but maybe there's nobody at her house to really listen to her. So understand what makes this chick tick, but don't give her the boot just yet.

★ The Gossip is frantic to make up for what she's missing—some importance, a feeling that she matters, and some super self-esteem—so she's grabbing at straws to get some. Understand that's what's driving her serious wish to dish, and give her some good news to spread.

★ Try to find the good in the Gossip, even if you have to look really hard. Maybe she's a great communicator but she hasn't found her niche yet. Otherwise, she'd use her talents for the good, not the bad. Can you subtly, or not so subtly, point her in the right direction?

RAPID RESPONSE: WHAT YOU SHOULD DO ABOUT THE GOSSIP

Want some quick tips when faced with a Gossip girl? Next time you find yourself in a sticky situation, try one of these:

★ When you find out someone's been gossiping about you, say, "I heard what you're saying about me. Thanks for being such a good publicist, and I love your price. It's free."

★ Just smile and say something like, "You know what they say: 'Those who can, do. And those who can't, gossip about it.' So carry on."

★ You and your gal pals can do an experiment to see how fast gossip spreads. Make up a rumor about yourselves and watch it spread like wildfire . . . then write an article for the school newspaper explaining what you found out. It will teach the entire school an interesting lesson.

And about that Ms. Backstabber? Well, first, don't tell her any more personal stuff about yourself or your friends. Just cool it with her and rely on your real friends. Real friends are trustworthy, loyal, respectful, goofy with you when you feel like it and serious when you need them to be, but most of all, they're dependable.

A REAL-LIFE STORY FROM MYA, 16

There's one girl in my neighborhood who has always done things in such a way that other girls found amusing. They'd laugh and talk and gossip about her behind her back all the time. It was like a sport or something. The worst thing they ever did to her was pretend to be her friend to her face. She never realized what they did to her. If she didn't do anything at all one day, they'd make up lies and spread them to all the kids.

During eighth grade, a few girls befriended the girl. They still talked junk behind her back. The girl was completely clueless and nobody ever told her the truth. The last week of school the girls pretended to get mad at the girl and didn't speak to her, and on the last day they planned to "jump" her, beat her up. But the girl's parents came to pick her up early and got there right as the fight was about to begin so, luckily, the girl was left unharmed.

Now that this girl is in high school, she found her own "crowd" and isn't picked on and when she is, she doesn't care. The other girls call her names like "slut, hoe, and bitch" when she walks by them, but it doesn't affect her anymore. She's every inch the winner!

Just last week she received an award for having the highest grade point average in eleventh grade.

Dr. Erika's Response

Awesome job! Pretty much on her own, this girl overcame the Gossips and the Backstabbers. That showed loads of courage and determination. Getting called nasty names the other girls dished out must have hurt. But instead of letting it get her down in the dumps, this girl rose above it. The fact is, she got stronger, and in the end, she showed them all. While the Gossips gabbed, this girl grabbed the opportunities. So she won out and the Gossips were the losers, and sore ones at that. My only wish is that someone gets those mean girls to stop it!

 NEW TEXT FROM CARLA, 16: Gossiping, spreading rumors, & name calling in school or online should have consequences that R spelled out like in a student handbook.

DEAR DIARY

It's time to fess up. Have you ever mindlessly repeated a juicy bit of gossip? Have you passed along some rumor and maybe even exaggerated it a little bit for that rush of power that comes from knowing something naughty about someone?

Or maybe you've participated in a gossip fest about a girl that you've always secretly envied, and now this blemish on her record—ha ha ha!—makes you feel better because it means she's not so superior after all. Right? Wrong. If you gossip about her and she doesn't about you, who's really superior?

So now it's time to think about your actions. Honestly, have you ever gossiped to your heart's content? Have you parroted something you heard about another girl because it gave you a thrill to have some inside info? Think of a time that you gossiped about a friend or classmate and write a few paragraphs or pages about it in your journal or your private blog.

Next, make a list of words that describe how you felt while you were doing it—powerful, popular. Or picky, pesky, petty, or guilty? And remember, be totally honest! You don't have anything to lose here, except maybe a bad attitude.

Look over the list and think about the words you chose to describe your feelings. What do they say about your personality? Now, imagine this scenario: You hear that the hottie you've been lusting after all year is interested in you. He's been asking some of your friends about you. When he asks what you're really like, they tell him—using all the bad words from your list. Yikes. How do you feel now?

Next, write about a time that you were the subject of gossip or rumors. This time, make a list of words that describe how being the subject of gossip made you feel. Probably not too good, huh? Now make a list of the words that describe what you thought of the girls who spread the gossip. How many match with the first list that you made about yourself? Then compare your lists and think about the type of person you would like to be. Are you happy with what you've written down, or could you use some improvement?

We all know that the rumor mill at school changes faster than Lady Gaga's look, but should you find yourself the target of the Gossip and her group, just remember to hold your head high and be proud of who you are. Don't let them get to you, and try to stay out of their range of fire. Better to devote your time to the friends who truly care about you!

FAB FIXES FOR WHATEVER ATTITUDE AILS YOU

The urge to blab something juicy—true or not—can creep into all of us once in a while. Gossiping about what celebs are doing, wearing, and baring is super fun and harmless. After all, we all love to talk about whom Taylor Swift is dating or what happened last night on *DWTS*. Likewise, getting the scoop at school about who's crushing on whom and who's doing what can be a blast.

It's common (and fun!) to engage in this kind of chit-chat sometimes. So if you do it rarely, good; but if it's an everyday occurrence, you'd better watch your back. This kind of gossipy attitude can easily morph into a bad habit that's hard to break. There may be days when your "blabbi-tude" takes over your life. Maybe you're ticked off that your best bud blew you off for her latest guy. Maybe you're seeking revenge on your little sister, so you jabber about her to your parents. Heck, maybe you just have a mean case of PMS. However, intentionally hurting others is very uncool. The next time you feel your claws coming out, try one of the following tips.

Rx: Countering Cattitude

Three times a day:

1. No matter how tempting it may be, don't give in to that mean-speaking streak that surfaces every so often. You've got better things to do with your time! So, don't let yourself be a part of the rumor factory. When someone tells you some juicy gossip, say, "Ah, verrry interesting." Then let it stop with you.

2. Spread nice rumors. That is, whenever you hear someone pass around something bad about a girl in your school, immediately pass around something way glowing about the same girl.

3. Go up to the girl who's being gossiped about and apologize to her. Make sure to tell her you don't believe a word of what's going around about her and that her life is no one else's business! A little bit of support goes a long way!

As for people gossiping about you, decide you won't let it get to you. You know you can ignore it, admit it's true, laugh it off, or best of all, be prepared for it. How?

By rehearsing all kinds of zinger-type answers, writing them down first, or inputting them in your personal computer lifestyle file and practicing them lots of times out loud. Here are some more possible retorts to girls gossiping about you:

★ "Oh, if only you knew. . . ."
★ "So what's your point?"
★ "If I could only talk. . . ."
★ "What else is new?"
★ "Really wish I could tell you the backstory, but on the advice of . . . oh, never mind."

Most of all, get busy doing what you love to do so you'll be moving ahead instead of gossiping behind the backs of your girlfriends. Don't let any mean chicks get in your way!

THE BOTTOM LINE

Here's what you have to remember about the Gossip:

★ She's dying for attention because she never got enough in the past or isn't getting enough now—at home or perhaps even at school. So she's trying to hog the limelight with her busy-bee blabber.
★ You really need to diss the dishing but not the source. The girl who's the biggest Gossip at school may be a verbal giant but a self-esteem midget. Feel for her, if you feel like it.

★ Always picture a Gossip as a popularity hound driven by attention hunger and sniffing for any juicy morsel to ease her hollow feeling. That way you know just how to act—you acknowledge her existence, understand her reasons, and then rise above her.

 You have one new e-mail: Though you may gain fame and popularity at the time you're gossiping on other girls, you won't even be remembered in a few days or weeks. After graduation, your fame is over, only the pain that you gave goes on and on. ~Hannah, 18

Chapter 3
The Teaser

In many ways, this mean queen—the Teaser—is much worse than the others. So many girls' lives have been ruined by her and her kind, and the worst thing is, she might not even know it! She could be your friend, your lab partner, your future college roommate, or your neighbor. The fact is, she's always around, and she could be a good friend . . . *if* you know how to handle her.

 You have one new e-mail: Many people use the phrase: Sticks and stones may break my bones, but words can never hurt me. Personally, I don't agree with that. At all! Words hurt people daily. Hurting words hurt so much. ~Amber, 15

This girl can scare you, and yet, she's actually good bud material. If she'd get help from someone—a classmate, teacher, coach, mom or dad, or from you!—she can turn out to be your best gal pal.

DEAR DR. ERIKA:

It started last year. This girl who used to be my best friend started being ill with me. She called me Goodyear blimp, big drawers, and all kinds of mean stuff. And any time a boy looked at me and I started talking to him, she made fun of him, too. Behind my back, this girl was and is even worse. She talks trash about me to all the other girls, none of which is true. I've tried to ignore her, but that hasn't done any good. It's getting so that I don't want to go to school anymore. Really, I don't know what to do.

~Tiana, 13

DEAR DR. ERIKA:

Let me come right out and say it: My complexion isn't as good as other girls'. Used to be it was awful, but now it's improving—a whole lot. Anyhow, when it was the pits, nobody mentioned it, but now that it's looking okay, my friends have started picking on me. See, a long time ago, we had a lesson about some bird called a sandpiper and I got the best grade on a report I did. Ever since, the other girls in class called me Ms. Sandpiper. Except my best friend—or who I thought was my best friend—changed "sandpiper" to "sandpaper" because of what my skin was like back then. They still call me Sandpaper wherever I go. And when we meet some new girls, like at church camp or wherever, my friend always introduces me as Sandpaper. I try to laugh it off, sure, and I try to call them names back, but it hurts. It really does.

~Zoe Yang, 15

FYI

So what exactly is teasing?

How can you identify the Teaser and her good buddy, the Name Caller? Are the Teaser's antics just cute chuckle provokers? Is name calling just joking around? Or is there venom beneath her seemingly innocent veneer? While the Teaser's actions may seem at first to be fun and games, in time the teasing escalates until you just can't take it anymore.

You have one new e-mail: DO NOT PICK ON PEOPLE. You never know how a person feels about herself or how far from the edge she is. ~LaKeisha, 14

To start, you may laugh and go along with all her jokes and jeering, but eventually you may hear a warning bell going off in your head. First, maybe she gives you a funny nickname, and you like it. You feel like she's adopted you as her friend. Next, maybe she rides you about the bad hair day you're having—heck, even you can admit when your 'do just won't cooperate. But next, maybe she starts picking on your shoes or clothes or the way you speak or sign your name on your notes or the way you look in the class picture posted on your school's website. And eventually, you find yourself flinching every time you pass her in the halls. You may feel hurt or even left out by her teasing, as if she's trying to make you feel bad for who you are. As if there's something really wrong with you!

 NEW TEXT FROM TEENA, 18: Girls pick at my accent. They say I talk "funny." My mom is from Miami and my dad is Puerto Rican. Of course that comes out in me, y wouldn't it?

It's time to stop this mean-chick chatter! Sometimes it's subtle, but most often it shows itself in all kinds of serious needling and verbal bullying. That can range from someone calling you a bad name because of your looks, smarts, size, religion, or ethnic background, because of your family, friends, background, or name, or the way you act, talk, or even walk. In other words, just about anything that might be a little different from others.

The Teaser comes in two basic formats:

1. Someone who's a friend who's just jealous of you and puts you down.
2. Someone you don't know that well who picks on you for seemingly no reason.

Yet whether they're close to you or not, it's hurtful to be teased. Oftentimes, this mean teasing is a way for someone who's hypercritical or envious of you to put you down. The Teaser often doesn't even realize why she's doing it, only that she is slick and quick with a quip and likes to show off her so-called verbal superiority and glibness.

Who knows? Maybe she could be a real friend if she could find a beneficial outlet for her verbal gifts—like freestyle poetry, public debate, or a teen blog. But for now, she's so fixated on making her classmates feel bad and spending lots of time and energy on verbally teasing and terrorizing them or on using technology to do so.

So if this "friend" always seems to use words, names, phrases, or what have you to make you feel bad, cool it with this fool. She's no friend at all! Actually, she may be worse than foolish. She may do some real serious harm. If her teasing goes unchecked, it can lead to a heck of a lot of trouble—viciousness, violence, total disaster, you name it.

UNIVERSAL HIGH SCHOOL

What people call Gloria when they see her in action at home is "smart." That she is, in addition to being 5'9", strong, athletic, and so pretty. Her dark-brown hair is thick and slightly wavy, so she can wear it in a messy ponytail, a half-and-half, or flat-ironed straight and glossy. Any way, it looks fabulous.

At home, it's not about her hair. Her mother died two years ago of breast cancer, and Gloria doesn't go a day without feeling an ache the size of a grapefruit inside her chest. That's why she's glad she has all this lame housework to do, so she doesn't have time to think.

Now her three younger brothers and her dad are all her responsibility. Whew—just the laundry is enough to scare you. Some of Dad's uniform stuff alone—he's a firefighter. Talk about a constant mess. And that's not all. All the guys in the neighborhood come over and watch every game on the 58" flat-screen TV with her dad. That means the house is a pigsty every day.

And what a noisy bunch—and all that backslapping and teasing. Some of it's even kinda lewd. They even pick on Gloria, her being the only female in the house. And sometimes her little brothers join in, too, even though she could kick their butts. They say, "What's the weather like up there?" because she's taller than some of them. Or they tease her about her cooking and criticize her constantly, even her hair.

Even though she wants to explode, she doesn't pick back at them—that will just make it worse. Still, they say, "Whatsa matter? Why aren't you like your papa? He's the funniest guy in Chicago."

Yeah, right. Maybe before Mama died. But now, when he's in his room late at night and thinks everyone's asleep, Gloria can hear him crying. Gloria doesn't cry, but she used to, not that it helped any. But now she's just angry most of the time. These anger fits grab a hold of her mostly at school when she sees all these other slick chicks who have it sooo easy. All they have to do is go to class and study, then home to rest, recoup, and relax. Chill at will—heck, Gloria wishes she could do likewise just one time!

As she hits the front entrance of school this day, she's actually feeling pretty good. She's already done two loads of stinky laundry and her hair looks perfect. "Hey, Squirt," she says to a tiny girl she sees. "Why don't you eat something once in a while, you Skinny Minnie?" she snaps at another. "What? You wearing a mop today?" she shouts and chuckles as she sees a third girl who has an unfortunate haircut. "Nice wig, loser."

By the time Gloria enters first period, she's teased a dozen girls, some of whom are actually her friends. So what? It's just for fun, right? If those prissy chicks can't take the heat, they should get the heck out of her way. And the same goes for her friends. If they're such good friends, why do they have to take everything so personally? Like Amy, who suddenly stopped talking to her because one day she made a crack about Amy's outfit. Why can't her friends understand that she's just teasing? After all, she has to put up with the same thing every night at home.

Knowing Gloria's background, perhaps it's understandable that Gloria has a tendency to pick on other girls at school. We can understand it, and perhaps at some point, we can forgive her for it, even though we may not like what she does. Knowing there are reasons for the actions of the Teaser doesn't necessarily lesson the pain.

In fact, teasing can have tragic consequences. Though most girls are stronger than they're given credit for, no one should have to tolerate constant teasing. Mean words can cut to the core. You might think to endure it is to cure it, but that's not the answer.

Besides, the more you put up with it, the bolder these mean taunts and teases can get. Instead of teasing less, the Teaser just keeps picking on and taunting other girls, getting more biting and bitter with each passing day.

Does any of this sound familiar to you? Are you a victim of the Teaser? Or perhaps you're one yourself? Remember, teasing is not okay—no matter what. So under no circumstances must you tolerate cruel, racial, sexist, or homophobic teasing of any kind, not of yourself, nor of any other girl. You have the power to put a stop to it. Right now.

 You have one new e-mail: People have always told me to do unto others as you would like them to do unto you. So I try hard to be nice to everyone. ~Taryn, 14

FAST QUIZ

The Teaser Test—How Well Do You Cope?

1. You've recently made friends with the new girl at school. At first, she seems cool and it seems like she's potential best-bud material. But lately she's been treating you badly, calling you names and stuff. You're starting to feel really weird around her, and you don't know what to do. Then, finally, she takes it too far and says some really embarrassing stuff to you at lunch right in front of your crush. You:

A. Try as best you can to keep your cheeks from flushing and wait for the torture to end. If you keep quiet, maybe she'll cut it out.

B. Laugh the loudest of anyone. After all, if your crush sees you've got such a charming sense of humor, maybe he'll ask you out.

C. Tell her she's not funny and point out that huge hunk of spinach between her two front teeth.

D. Let her know that she's pushing it and try to steer the subject away from any potentially embarrassing subject matter. Later, when you're alone, you'll have a talk with her and let her know that you don't consider her actions acceptable.

2. On the bus ride home, the Teaser and her gang have been picking on a girl who's really quiet and always sits by herself. Each day, she bolts off the bus with tears in her eyes. You:

A. Turn up your headphones and ignore the situation. It's a jungle out there, and you'd rather not get involved.

B. Snag a seat next to the Teaser and try to join in— better to be the teaser than the teased! Besides, that girl they're teasing is a nobody, anyway.

C. Carefully plan your attack. You can't stand a chick with a bad 'tude, and the Teaser and her friends have one! You'll teach them a lesson and maybe that other girl will be able to leave the bus with a smile.

D. Try snagging the seat next to the girl who's being picked on and talk to her—there's safety in numbers, and you're not so concerned with what the Teaser and her group have to say. If you show them they're not bugging you, they'll probably back off in a few days, anyway.

3. For some reason, you just can't get the Teaser and her friends off your back! Every day for the past week, they've been saying mean stuff as you pass by the second-floor water fountain, their usual hangout. To make matters worse, you found an "anonymous" note in your locker this morning that reiterates all of the things they've been teasing you about. You:

A. Choose another route so you don't have to go by them in the hall.

B. Spend the weekend trying to fix whatever it is they've been picking on. If you can fix whatever it is they hate about you, maybe they'll stop bothering you.

C. Gather all of your best girl buds together and write a rebuttal note pointing out everything that is wrong with the Teaser and her group, and then some. What the heck—it's best to fight fire with fire.

D. Take a strong stance. You're a strong girl, so look them in the eye and say, "Is that the best you can do? Getting your kicks out of teasing people? I really feel sorry for you." Then walk off with your head held high, on to more important things.

4. You're in yearbook class, which meets after school, and you just handed in a layout to a girl who is two grades ahead of you. She takes one look at your work, breaks out laughing, and calls the rest of the yearbook staff together, pointing out every mistake you made. You:

A. Nod like a bobble-head doll, saying, "You're so right, I'm so dumb, this was really stupid—will you give me another chance, please?" then sneak into the hall and wipe your watery eyes, vowing to somehow drop this class or be sick a lot.

B. Say, "Oh you're so right! I don't know why I never thought of that before. I can change it if you want—right now. Maybe I can model it after one of your layouts? Please? You're so talented!"

C. Say, "Listen, Bigmouth, my layout rocks, and you know it. Maybe if you spent more time studying and less time brushing out your messy hair, you wouldn't have flunked your trig exam, so back off!"

D. Say, "Thanks for the comments. I know you're trying to help, but I got these ideas from the award-winning yearbook the school across town has done. It's time we updated the dinosaur designs we've always used and put our school on the map. Look, I've got to run—swim team meets in fifteen minutes. I'll e-mail you later—I have awesome ideas for the cover."

Now it's time to find out how you did. Total up your answers.

ANSWERS

If you answered mostly As: Hey, girl! Hold that head up as high as you can! Since when does ignoring a problem make it go away? While there's nothing wrong with staying out of the way of trouble, there is something to be said for standing up for yourself. So do it. Think of all the good things you have in your life, and remember, this is just a brief moment in time. If you don't start making a difference for yourself now, how will you ever become the superstar you were meant to be?

If you answered mostly Bs: You're letting the other girls label you and make fun of you. You have so much potential to do great things, why would you try to change who you are because of the whims of the Teaser? You spend too much time trying to adapt yourself to suit the Teaser's tastes, and let's face it, if she had any taste at all she wouldn't spend so much time putting you down. Try doing something that you love in order to please yourself. You'll soon find yourself walking through life with a whole new outlook.

If you answered mostly Cs: You're not afraid to put the smack-down on the Teaser when she's getting on your case or the cases of other girls. But don't go patting yourself on the back just yet. Beating the Teaser at her own game a time or two will definitely help put her in her place, but you're not here to stir up trouble. Sometimes, challenging the Teaser stirs up more trouble than it's worth.

If you answered mostly Ds: On a bad day, the Teaser definitely gets to you, but it's okay. You've got enough class to know when to stand up for yourself and when those boots were made for walkin'! Maybe you can take your smarts a step further, if you wish. Why not try to stop the teasing of other girls at your school? There are plenty of things you can do to stop it, just wait and see!

If you have a mixture of As, Bs, Cs, and Ds: Review all of the above. Obviously, there's a little bit of everything in you, which is great. Now, can you work on having a little more of that Answer-D attitude?

TEASER SMARTS: WHAT SHOULD YOU KNOW ABOUT THE TEASER?

While the Teaser and close cronies can have complex reasons for acting like they do, you run across them in just about any class or group of girls. Here's how to pick them out of a crowd:

★ The Teaser feels bad about herself: Maybe she's not getting any respect at home or nobody has ever made her feel worthwhile or she's constantly teased and criticized herself. As a result, she's trying to drag you down in the gutter where she feels she is.

★ Remember, by belittling something in you or about you or about your background, family, and friends, she wants to climb out of the hole she feels she's in.

★ Even the worst Teaser or Name Caller can break her mean habits. It may take some time, but if you feel like it, try to befriend the Teaser. Maybe with your help she will improve.

RAPID RESPONSE: WHAT YOU SHOULD DO ABOUT THE TEASER

So now that you know about the Teaser, what can you do about her? Try these tactics:

1. The first time someone teases you, say, "Funny, ha-ha-ha," but with a serious face. The second time, say, "You said the exact same thing yesterday. What's wrong? Are you okay?" Act real concerned. The third time, input in your phone word for word what's being said, by whom, when, and where. When someone asks, "What're you doing?" reply, "I'm documenting what's going on." This might get some laughs, but it will stop most of the serious teasing on the spot. Trust me.

2. If the Teaser keeps it up, carry a small tape recorder and ask the mean chick, "Would you mind repeating what you just said? I just want to make sure I have you quoted accurately." Then tape her slurs, bad words, and names, whatever she has to say. Even better if all of a sudden she doesn't have anything to say.

3. But if the teasing persists to a point where you really can't take it anymore and your smart-girl tactics aren't working as you thought they would, maybe it's time to share your problems with someone else who can help. Talk to someone you trust—a teacher, guidance counselor, or even your mom or dad. Pretend you're a lawyer and think of it as a case you're going to handle. But don't bluff; really resolve to solve the problem.

 You have one new e-mail: Whenever someone calls me a name, I just say, "Stop it." If they do it again, I repeat, "Stop it!" The third time, I'm either in the office or talking to the guidance counselor about it. ~Debbie, 16

Should the teasing atmosphere at your school continue there are some crucial things you can do to teaseproof your school. Organize a group of girls who are sick of the teasing and name calling and the consequences. Familiarize yourself with your school's bullying policy and then form a club dedicated to upholding it.

Choose a cool name for your group and then find a teacher you're close to who will sponsor your group. Think of yourselves as the updated *Charlie's Angels* of your school—battling evil in whatever form it comes. You can plan weekly meetings, get speakers to come, make presentations about the effects of bullying, and maybe even network with other high schools.

Letting teasing happen to someone around you and not stopping it just isn't cool. Take a look at the examples below. If Rose and Julia still remember the incidents, you can bet the victims remember them, too.

 NEW TEXT FROM SONYA, 19: I think, sadly, everyone has experienced some kind of teasing or taunting from kids their age. I have been a victim of it. I still get nightmares.

Rose remembers: "Last year at an assembly, the whole school was in the gym and this girl came in walking kind of strange and the whole school went into an uproar of laughter and rude comments. And they kept rehashing this for weeks. Sometimes I wonder how that girl felt and whatever happened to her."

What good is it to think later about how embarrassed and bad a girl who was teased might have felt? No good at all! For even though the girl may have acted like it didn't bug her, we all know it did.

And who knew how this girl felt: "There was this girl in English class who had long and wild hair. One girl called her 'Mop Top,' and we all started laughing. Sure it was funny, but nobody thought how embarrassed the girl might have been," Julia recalls.

Labels are for soup cans and sunscreens, not for people. By labeling others around you, you aren't giving them a fair shake because you aren't letting yourself see them for who they really are. Instead, you're creating a false image of them. Picture branding cattle with a hot poker—that's the way it feels to a girl who gets called an awful name day after day after day. You never want to cause anyone pain.

A REAL-LIFE STORY FROM JENNIFER, 18

When I was in eighth grade, there was a tiny girl who was cross-eyed and wore thick glasses. She was always so sad because the other girls picked on her about her glasses: "Four Eyes, Four Eyes!" they said or "Man, she's blind as a bat!" She was horrified to go to school every day and face these cruel girls. She would cry and tell her parents she felt bad so she wouldn't have to go to school.

This continued for a couple of years until it got so bad that the tiny girl cried at school. This made the bullies tease her even worse. She had very few friends that were really nice to her because those mean girls would pick on them, too.

Then in tenth grade the girl asked her mother to get her contact lenses to help solve her problem.

Today this girl is one of the best, most popular cheerleaders in the school. She overcame her tormentors and the tough issues she had to deal with every day in middle school. Quite a few younger girls look up to her now because she found it inside of herself to forgive those girls who had hurt her so badly for so long. She thinks that the things she went through have made her a better person in the long run, and she never picks on anyone because of something they can't help. I'm just so proud of this girl who just happens to be my younger sister.

Dr. Erika's Response

This girl persevered, and didn't let teasing ruin her life. Instead, she became stronger. I'm sure having a big sister like Jennifer helped her, too. Can you think of someone from your school who has overcome a similar obstacle? Who knows, maybe that person was even you! Keeping positive, even in the face of hard situations, can help you survive and thrive. Mean teasing hurts, but just try to remember that those cruel words only have meaning if you let them. The Teaser is using these tactics to make herself feel better, but you don't have to let her get you down.

 You have one new e-mail: Is it really worth breaking down someone's self-esteem and confidence just so you can look big and bad for a few minutes? ~Vickie, 17

DEAR DIARY

Now it's time to think about what you can do to prevent teasing. For starters, there is no greater comfort (not even your favorite jeans!) than knowing you are not alone. Teasing has been around for eons, and it will probably never stop completely. However, you can use your girl power to give support to your friends and classmates. Try this little exercise below. You can do it just for yourself, or, if you want to, you can share it with others. It's your call. So, take a survey of ten, twenty, or even 100 girls in your school. Ask them if they have ever been the victims of teasing. Then ask them how it made them feel.

Then get your creative juices flowing. Write an article about teasing and how it has affected you and the girls in your school. Write as if you're a magazine reporter and your words will reach thousands of people—because they can. First, start with a rough draft in your trusty journal or log, but ask yourself how many girls could be helped this way. If you like what you've come up with, maybe you can post it on a website or publish it in your school paper or maybe even send it off to your favorite magazine. If not, you can keep it for yourself to read a few years from now or maybe even to share with your own children someday.

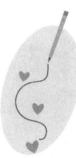

 NEW TEXT FROM CARINNA, 16: Being called a name and made fun of is the worst feeling in the whole world. It hurts!

FAB FIXES FOR WHATEVER ATTITUDE AILS YOU

Have you ever teased anyone? A classmate, a friend, your little sister? If so, you pretty much did the normal thing. We all like to do a little kidding now and then. I kid you not!

So, if the kidding is good-natured, infrequent, and nobody minds, then that's okay. It's always fun to laugh and kid with friends—it can even be a form of affection.

But keep in mind that the line between harmless kidding and hurtful teasing is a fine one, so be sure to watch yourself. If you find that you've been teasing in a sarcastic or snide, negative way, maybe it's because you're developing a negative attitude about yourself. Just because you're having a rotten day doesn't mean that you should try to make others have a rotten day, too. So whenever you are tempted to show a nasty attitude, in other words a nasty-tude, that makes you say stuff that's rude, do something to counteract it.

Rx: Nixing Nasty-tude

The next time you feel a case of Nasty-tude coming on:

1. Turn the nasty into nice. Rather than letting nasty words come out of your mouth, make it a point to compliment those around you. Do it more than once—you'll be amazed at the response.
2. If you do find yourself with a bad case of nasty-tude, apologize immediately to anyone you've picked on. Tell her you're sorry and you won't do it again. And mean it.
3. Whenever you feel the urge to tease, immediately do something that makes you feel better, like taking a walk, stretching, breathing in deeply, and saying a favorite word three times, like, "Love-love-love." By then, your mean gene will have taken a hike.

THE BOTTOM LINE

The bottom line about teasers is to remember the following:

★ Deep down the Teaser isn't pleased with herself.
★ Don't forget, the Teaser is insecure. Her cure for that is trying her best to make you and others insecure, too. Don't take the Teaser's biting barbs

as personal. From this moment on, put a shield around yourself that deflects her verbal arrows. This shield, made of your know-how, will empower you against the Teaser.

★ Help other girls around you arm themselves with this shield, too. Do it as soon as you notice another girl being teased because you might not get a second chance. And you don't want to carry the burden of not having done something—small or big—to stop the verbal bullying or cyber bullying when you could have. Remember, the time to stop it is now; tomorrow may be too late.

So whenever there's a culture of the vultures at your school, closing your eyes and shutting your ears is no way to solve the problem, for yourself or for others. You must be courageous. And you can be. Please be the heroine for the underdog. Be as strong as you can, and right the wrong.

 You have one new e-mail: One thing to remember is that the girls you act nasty to are usually some of the nicest girls you could meet and would give you the shirts off their backs. Tormenting other girls therefore deletes another terrific person from the list of your potential friends. ~Dianne, 18

Chapter 4
The Bully

She's defiant, outspoken, and tough. She may run alone or with her pack, and she seems to get her kicks out of being cruel to smaller or weaker people. You've probably seen her—throwing hateful stares at classmates, whispering threats as you walk past her in the hall, or maybe even hitting or pushing you out of the way when she thinks no one else is looking. You've just encountered the Bully. But read on, for this chick who's so tough on the outside might not really be what she seems.

 You have one new e-mail: Once the bullies push a girl to the edge, she has a wish for revenge, or more commonly, an urge to escape. She wants the pain to end one way or another. She does what she can to make it stop. ~Kerri, 16

DEAR DR. ERIKA:

I hate school—like, really hate it. Every time I pass by this tall mean-looking girl in the hall, she punches me hard—I got the bruises to show you. But nobody listens to me. My mother, she says to just take another stairway and then what happens? My teacher writes me up 'cause I'm late. And I don't even know the girl! Why is she so mean?

~Anika, 16

DEAR DR. ERIKA:

I've always been good at sports, and I've played on my school team with older girls since seventh grade. But lately I'm beginning to dread going to practice. There is another girl my age who's really tall and she's way mean. Not when the coach is looking—oh no, then she's all goody-goody. But when he steps out of the gym to get his mail from the main office and we have the run of the place to ourselves, then she intentionally hits me with her elbow. Or she runs smack into me. She always grins from ear to ear—excuse me, excuse me!—but I'm not fooled. I know she's trying to hurt me till I quit. So maybe that's what I should do, but I love basketball. I mean just look at those Duke University girls, how great they are. That's what I see when I close my eyes. But then I think about those bruises and the bullying and I feel horrible. Why does this girl hate me so much?

~Charlotte, 14

FYI

Now this is one scary chick. Her actions ruin school for so many girls by haunting the hallways and stairwells, just waiting to cause trouble. Even if you're not the target of the  Bully, it's inevitable that you'll run into her, whether you want to or not. The Bully has it in for other girls, that's for sure! You've probably experienced her in action—cursing out other girls, "accidentally" bumping into them or making them drop their books, or stealing their stuff. When confronted by a teacher, the Bully says with a saccharine smile, "Oh, I just borrowed that. No big deal."

It's not hard to figure out that the Bully is trying to hurt you. Maybe you don't even like going to school anymore because you're constantly on the lookout for her. She and her gang can pop up anywhere—in the halls, stairways, and bathrooms—and it's never good news when you spot her. There will always be some violent acts, small or large, or the threat of it hanging in the air when the Bully is roaming around.

Of all the types of mean chicks, the Bully is probably the toughest one to handle because she uses physical violence. No matter what physical things she's doing to you— from a small shove in the hallway to a nearly invisible punch on the arm—it's violence and it's wrong!

Violence in girls can have many different causes, and those causes can be really hard to put into words. Your job isn't to find out what causes the violence, but to not let the Bully get in the way of your happiness or peace of mind. As you've probably figured out by now, there are no magic words to make the Bully go away, no happy after-school-special ending to her story. But there are a few things that you can do to empower yourself. The list below provides three things you can do to handle this behavior. It's not as complicated as you might think, but it does require you to be brave. Okay, here goes:

1. Stop being a victim.
2. Help others stop being victims.
3. Do your best to speak out and stop the terrorizing that's ruining school for so many girls.

So remember these simple words: No more! It's got to stop. And it will, right now, with you.

Bullying breeds bullying and violence breeds violence. Once it's tolerated, it only gets worse, more widespread, more ingrained, and uglier. If the behavior of the Bully and her crew is left unchecked, you might even see some of the girls from previous chapters—the Snob, the Gossip, and the Teaser—pick up bullying behavior.

 NEW TEXT FROM LEILA, 14: There r so many girls who are the victims of bullying peers. It happens after school—they get scratched, pinched, have their hair pulled, or are spit at—4 no reason except just being there.

Bullying is a problem in just about every school. And even though many schools are now aware of the problem, it still goes on not only during regular class time but also after school when girls participate in all their fun extracurricular activities.

But there's no fun with the Bully around. Not when you have to take the long way to your destination, say, the gym for a meeting to plan floats for the homecoming parade. How can you enjoy going to a club meeting when you are scared you might run smack into the Bully and her bad buds? Nowhere on the school grounds is safe!

Many Bullies may have a background of dysfunction or violence at home. In other words, something went wrong with their lives or families early on. So they've learned to be cruel or lash out at others as a form of self-defense. Because they have been injured, they want to injure you. Bullies often come from homes where they're cursed at or beaten or simply ignored.

> ✉ **You have one new e-mail:** Throughout my life there have been many times that I looked down on myself and cried. This was all the cause of other girls bullying me. They pushed me or elbowed me aside every chance they got. I don't know how many times I ended up with a bruise. ~Niqua, 14

UNIVERSAL HIGH SCHOOL

Kelli is a pretty sixteen-year-old with stunning blue eyes and light brown hair cut in a cool, short style. Everybody knows her because she's a star athlete at UHS. She holds the record for most points scored in a girls' basketball game, and that's just one of her sports.

But what people don't know about Kelli would surprise them. Kelli's parents died in a car crash when she was just two years old. She spent the next five years of her life being shuffled from one relative to another until she ended up in a foster home with a bunch of older girls who bullied her. Nothing serious at first, just a kick or two in the shin under the table at supper. When her foster mother asked Kelli why her legs were always so bruised she wanted to speak up, but the bigger girls threatened Kelli. Kelli shrugged off the pain; she had to. The kicking escalated to outright beatings and the threat of more beatings if she ever told, so she could never tell anyone.

She felt so alone, but at least she had something she could cling to—her new puppy. However, it turned out that her foster parents were allergic to dogs, so they gave the puppy away, despite Kelli's tearful begging and pleading.

All this stuff happened years ago, of course. One by one, the other girls moved out and Kelli was finally left on her own with her foster parents.

Of course, Kelli's life is better now. She's at Universal High and making pretty good grades. She has her own crew—girls like her, who came from tough situations and still made it— not one wimp or wuss among them. And they rule the school; no other girl better mess with them and everyone knows it.

Kelli is the boss of the gang, natch. Every day, on her way to practice, she clatters down the stairs, scattering all of the girls who happen to be walking up, just to keep up her image.

She shoves them aside, and if any nosy newcomer gapes at her, she knocks them out of her way. She smiles at the rush of power she feels as she watches them cower. All these lame sissies, she thinks. She wishes she could get rid of them all.

Kelli's on the varsity basketball team and doing real well, but the coach keeps warning her about not getting into fights at practice. Even though she's the star player, the fighting is affecting her record. Coach has been cutting her some slack, but lately Kelli has the feeling that she's been pushing it too far. She almost got in major trouble for that fistfight in the lunchroom the other day, and it almost cost her playing in the game this weekend! While basketball is a great way for Kelli to work off some of her anger, taking it out on girls in the hallways or on the court is not cool. Luckily, Kelli has her coach watching out for her. But not all girls have a parent or teacher or coach keeping tabs on them.

You have one new e-mail: Usually, I like to be as peaceful as possible, but sometimes I do get a real urge to hurt other girls in some way, either by kicking them or slapping them. But what I have to do is overcome those hateful feelings. ~Jana, 15

As she waits for practice, Kelli decides to start on her English homework. It's a free write, meaning she gets to pick her own topic. Kelli enjoys the assignment, describing in vivid detail that last basketball game when she scored 24 points. Basketball is her passion, and she is surprised how easily the words come out.

As she finishes, however, Kelli's smile turns to a frown. At the bottom of the page, she scribbles in the smallest handwriting possible: *Sometimes, I think about killing myself!* And then quick as a wink, she erases it.

Jana is right to recognize that she needs to overcome those hateful feelings, but that can't always be done alone. Some girls have so many things to deal with that getting at the root of their anger, which is often the basis of physical bullying, can be tough if they try to do it without getting outside help. Indeed, if you or someone you know is trying to tackle feelings of anger that don't go away, it may be best to seek help from adults whom you trust. It's natural to be angry at times, like when you have the kind of day where you miss the school bus, forget your biology homework, and halfway through your first period your hair decides to freak out. But when that anger becomes uncontrollable or overshadows everything else in your life, it's best to turn to someone who can help.

 NEW TEXT FROM VERONICA, 17: Every girl takes her anger out in different ways—some in money wasting, some in food gorging, and some in beating up on other girls.

True, and since there are so many angry girls around, you need a quick way to find out if you're at risk in your school.

FAST QUIZ

Bully Battles—Are You a Victim?

1. The school cafeteria is jam-packed. Because of an assembly earlier, all grade levels have the same lunch hour, leaving no empty tables for latecomers. You've managed to snag one of the last remaining tables for you and your friends, who are still in the lunch line, but the Bully and her crew decide they want this table. She marches up to it, kicks your chair, and snaps, "Move it. Now!" You:

   A. Get the heck out of there—fast! Maybe you can sit on the floor or squeeze in with another table. Or huddle against the janitor closet.

   B. Hop up, dust off the seat, and bring her a linen napkin and a crystal water glass—anything to make her dining experience a fine one!

   C. Say, "No problem, I was just leaving." As you stand up, you "accidentally" overturn your lunch tray and dump the remaining cafeteria gruel all over the Bully.

   D. Say, "I see that you're way upset. You know, I think the guidance office has an after-school anger-management program for people like you. Why don't you go check it out? Meanwhile, this is my seat and I'm not leaving."

2. You've been assigned a research paper on Shakespeare and you're in the library doing some online research. There are only a dozen computer stations, but your teacher posted a schedule, and this is your allotted time. The Bully strides in, hovers over you, and snaps, "Outta my way. I got stuff to do, you know." You:

A. Flutter away as fast as your Uggs will take you, losing all of your research in the process. The Bully always gets her way, no matter what, so it's easier just to let her take over. You can always come back during study hall or lunch and start over again.

B. You're practically a computer genius, and you know the Bully hardly knows her password. This is your chance to finally get on her good side. Not only do you graciously give up your computer, but you also offer to help her do her research . . . and her report. And any other assignments she may have.

C. Tell her you'll get up when your time is up and not a nano-second sooner, then turn your back and continue with your work. You even stay seven and a half minutes past your allotted time, just to mess with her. As an added bonus, before you sign off, you make sure to jam the printer and unplug the mouse. Heck, she never makes your life easy—and revenge is so so sweet!

D. Say in a firm, loud voice, "Please, don't interrupt me again!" Then go on with your work. When the Bully hovers over you, glaring, you point to the posted schedule and say, "If you want the schedule changed, why don't you see Mrs. Smith? She's right over there."

3. After school, you're on your way to an important meeting to plan the annual school fair. You've been looking forward to serving on the committee all year. Bummer that you run into the Bully on the staircase and she's in the mood for trouble. She blocks the staircase leading down to the walkway that connects the main building to the gym. You:

A. Try to smile and move around her, but she just won't let you by, so you turn and slink back up the steps, out the door, and head home. It's just not worth the trouble. Besides, there will be tons of girls at the meeting anyway, and they don't need you and your silly suggestions. No one will even miss you.

B. Compliment her on her outfit, haircut, shoes, whatever. After all, they say flattery will get you everywhere. Once you get her talking about herself, you can slip past her, down the stairs, and to your meeting. Besides, if you score points with her now, maybe she won't bug you so much in the future.

C. Get in her face. Your momma didn't raise no scaredy-cat, not by a long shot. Too bad a teacher breaks it up before things get ugly, but you think, "Let the word go out to everybody—don't mess with me, sister!"

D. Meet her gaze directly and say, "Excuse me," making sure your tone is polite yet firm. If she still won't let you by, you make a choice. You can continue to confront her in a mature and confident way, willing to face whatever may happen, or you can turn around and take a different, Bully-free route to the meeting. Meanwhile, text your friend who is at the meeting to let her know that you're unavoidably delayed.

4. You're at the bus stop outside of your school when the Bully and her gang show up and "accidentally" bump into you. You:

A. Apologize and move a few steps away from them. When that doesn't work, you call or text your mom for a ride. Public transportation isn't what it used to be, and you don't mind waiting two hours for your mother to come. It's a good time to catch up on your math work.

B. Laugh along and try to join in their conversation. Maybe if you can join in on their banter, they'll include you instead of being rude to you.

C. Yell, "Do it again, I dare you!" as loud as you can so everyone around you stops and stares. The Bully looks startled and takes a step back. While you have everyone's attention you yell, "Yeah, that's right, back away! It's what you do best anyway!"

D. Throw her a sideways glance and step quietly away from the Bully and her friends. You act like it was an accidental bumping—the first time—but you still move away from the Bully and close to a teacher or supervisor. If the same thing happens again, you'll probably take more serious steps, but for now, it's better to leave it alone.

Now it's time to find out how you did. Total up your answers.

ANSWERS

If you answered mostly As: We know the Bully can be scary, but you're letting her control your life, and that's holding you back from doing what you want to do when you want to do it. Why let the Bully dictate your actions? She's just a thorn in the side of the entire student body, and she's the one who needs to shape up or ship out, not you. So, get on with your life and get on the ball. You have the right to walk anywhere you like.

If you answered mostly Bs: Who are you, someone's slave? Stop kowtowing to every whim of the Bully. By always doing what she says, you're making the situation worse for you and for others. Your fearful actions are enabling the Bully to keep on bullying, and that's not cool. No matter what you may think, the Bully is not your friend. Why would you want a friend that treats you like dirt, anyway? Next time, take a stand and be yourself. It's time to make a change!

If you answered mostly Cs: Okay, so you may have stopped the Bully at her game a time or two. You're definitely not afraid to stand up for yourself.

You have so much power, and now you just have to learn how to use it, not abuse it. Your actions make you more and more like the Bully, instead of the special, strong-willed, and determined girl you really are. Imitating bad behavior isn't the way to solve problems, so don't get caught in that dangerous pattern. You have the power to make the Bully back down, so be smart, and make a fresh start—no more Bully behavior for you!

If you answered mostly Ds: You're focused on your own agenda, and there's plenty to do without worrying about the Bully and her antics. Your life is an open road, and the Bully is like one of the bumps along your way—you just move around her and get on with your life. If you can't get her off your back, you know what to do: Tell her to stop it now, or you'll find a way to stop it yourself. You're on the right track, so just continue to let your girl power shine! Don't let anyone get in your way—ever.

If you have a mixture of As, Bs, Cs, and Ds: Review all of the answers. Obviously, there's a little bit of everything in you, which is great. Now, can you work on having a little more of that D attitude?

Even though more and more teachers and adults are realizing the problems the Bully and her crew can cause, it's definitely not something that will go away overnight. In fact, the Bully problem is still spreading, even as you read this.

You have one new e-mail: At our middle school, girls who smile and enjoy school get picked on. People say things like they have a "Kool-Aid" smile and that they are weird, and then they shove them "accidentally." Yeah, right. These kinds of mean comments and all that pushing and shoving can really lower a girl's self-esteem and make her hate school. ~Janeen, 13

And what starts in middle school usually continues into high school, where what was just an instance of a little shoving here and there can escalate to scary proportions. It can even turn the girls who were bullied into real mean chicks.

Without solutions for girls who are the victims of bullying, a vicious cycle starts. Things quickly go from bad to worse, and that's so unfair! You and your group of friends need an environment that's totally safe and geared to your success.

BULLY SMARTS: WHAT SHOULD YOU KNOW ABOUT THE BULLY?

So how can you stop the mean chicks and negative cliques and nix their dirty tricks? Arm yourself with the following info on the Bully:

★ Even though the Bully causes problems for you, you aren't the cause of her problems. By understanding this, you empower yourself to start on a path of positive change that will continue for years to come.

★ Most bullies come from an environment where they were bullied or abused themselves; when they bully you, they're imitating the way they were raised. This is too bad, but it doesn't excuse their behavior.

★ Bullies may feel insecure or unloved and have little or no confidence. Often their self-esteem is very low. By bullying you, they're just trying to make themselves feel better, but that's not going to work. You're not their punching bag!

When faced with the Bully head on, try one of these options:

1. While it won't work forever, avoiding the Bully as much as possible is one option until you've figured out exactly what to do.

2. Next, change your attitude toward the Bully. You can handle her better than you think! You can start by going to school each day strong and prepared, instead of scared and intimidated. Have a Bully proof comment ready, such as, "I'm sorry you're having a bad day!" Then step around her and carry on as usual.

3. Stand up for yourself! If the Bully is bothering you, tell her to cut it out. If the bullying continues, say, "I told you to stop it or else." Many Bullies are cowards; once she sees that you're taking a stand, she'll probably back down.

WHAT I WENT THROUGH—A REAL-LIFE STORY FROM LAROSA, 16

During my whole childhood, I was a very self-conscious person. I was often criticized for my appearance. I had a small number of friends and acquaintances. In seventh grade, there was a group of girls that thought they were bad. They walked around acting like no one could ever step in their way at any time, and like they could get any boy whenever they wanted. I was a girl they hated because I wasn't as pretty or the same size as them. I was overweight and wore glasses, and when I passed them, they hit me every time. They slapped me, and punched me, and pushed me down the stairs like I was nothing.

One of the girls in this group was once my friend when we were younger. She had made up her mind that I was unfit to be her friend, so she stopped talking to me. Another girl in the group was my cousin, and we didn't talk because she didn't like me.

Not much later, there was a talent show coming up. So me and my friends tried to figure out what our performance would be. I decided to sing, with my friends doing the backup, and the group of mean chicks came up with a dance.

Finally, it was time for the big audition. I made it through, but the mean chicks' dance was cut. After two practices, it was time for the real talent show. I sang my heart out that night and all of my family was so proud.

Even the group of mean girls was there, jealous because I made it into the talent show. They made faces and laughed while I sang, but I ignored them. When I was finished, I got a standing ovation, so I bowed and then left the stage. My mother was in tears and I was sooo happy. After that, it was time for the judges to announce the winner.

Third place was given to one of my friends. Second place went to a girl who was a ballerina. When it was time for first place, I felt chills go up my spine. And when they announced that the first place winner was me, I was thrilled. I ran and hugged my mom and family. Then I went to get my prize of $100.

The group of mean girls came up and tried to start a conversation, but I just turned my back and hugged my friends. There was no need to say anything—I was a winner!

Dr. Erika's Response

LaRosa, you were so strong in the face of all those mean chicks trying to pull you down. They treated you so badly, but you didn't let it get to you and destroy you. Instead, you clung to your dream and worked for it; in other words, you persevered. You were a winner even before you won the big talent show. Congratulations!

 NEW TEXT FROM CAITLIN, 17: Being constantly dissed by other girls when I was younger made me who I am today—an achiever.

DEAR DIARY

Now it's time to get real with yourself. Have other girls ever treated you meanly? Or have you seen one of your friends suffer because of other girls? When did it happen? What were the circumstances? Maybe someone forced you to give up your seat on the bus or cut in front of you in line or hit you or physically hurt you in some way. Surely, these things hurt you. But you probably couldn't express how much it hurt while you were in school. Well, now it's time to get those feelings out.

Write about one of those instances and how it made you feel. Don't hold back! It's okay to cry or feel angry or both. That's what your journal or blog is for. Next, write down how you over-came that feeling—spell it all out. Did you fight back? Did you walk away? What exactly did you do? How do you feel about how you handled it?

And finally, make a list of other ways that you could have handled the situation. Was there some-thing you could have done differently? Better? Keep these things in mind for next time. Make a second list, this time as if you were writing it for younger girls who find themselves in the crosshairs of the Bully. What advice would you give them? Remember, no one is judging you here, so just write away. Your writing is all for you. By using your journal, you are revealing the real strength in you.

FAB FIXES FOR WHATEVER ATTITUDE AILS YOU

Some days, you get up on the wrong side of the bed; you just don't feel like yourself. You don't mean to, but you snarl and bark and sling things and fling words, some of them nasty. On days like that you may slam doors a little louder than usual, or when you drop your books on your desk, you may do it with an extra bang! And oh my, how you heave those exaggerated sighs.

Though your anger doesn't last forever, sometimes you're just mad because something doesn't go your way. It might be some dumb little thing or bigger stuff that ticks you off: You get a zit when you're trying to look your best or you get your period at exactly the wrong moment or you have that teacher who's always calling on you the moment you don't know something. It's easy to take your anger out on others when you're feeling this way. Maybe it's too easy!

And suddenly all the little mean things other girls have done to you get on your nerves and get blown way out of proportion. You feel like the world doesn't like you, and you want to get everybody back, starting with your little brother, older sister, or maybe even your best friends. You feel like lashing out or punching something or someone or kicking something or someone in the butt. Why is everything going wrong today?

So how can you handle it? What can you do on days when you have a real bad attitude or a real mad-itude?

Rx: Mastering Mad-itude

The next time you feel mad-itude coming on, try doing the following:

1. Say as little as possible, because you know once you open your little trap, you're more likely to snap. Not cool.
2. Give people around you a fair warning. From parents to teachers to your best buds, it's better to let them

know your 'tude isn't what it should be. Say, "I'm having a bad day. Can we please discuss this tomorrow?"

3. As soon as you get home from school, go for the comfort. You know what makes you feel better. Cuddle up in a soft blanket, kick off your Converse, listen to your favorite play list, and unwind for a bit. Later, if that mad-itude has begun to fade, maybe make that quick dash into your favorite store and do some browsing—maybe even buy something new.

4. Try to always have something fun planned. The madder you get, the better your plans should be—after first getting your mom's permission, of course. So make something that rocks happen to you on a mad day. In no time, your mad-itude will turn into glad-itude; you'll stop pouting and spouting off.

You're in charge of your life, your happiness, and your moods! While sometimes you can't help but brood, just make sure it doesn't last.

THE BOTTOM LINE

Here's what you need to remember about Bullies:

★ There are lots of Bullies in the world. They're up to no good, but now you can deal with them because now you know what drives them. You understand that their actions don't have to do with you, but with their own problems.

★ It's okay to feel sorry for the Bully and the things she's had to endure, but that shouldn't be your primary focus. Your main goal is to empower yourself and, through that, start a trend that stops the bullying.

★ Be strong, devise a plan of action, and see it through. First, tell the Bully to stop—loud and clear. If she doesn't stop, take action. Get your friends together, stand up to the Bully, and let her know you are not afraid. Finally, if the bullying persists and you really need a solution, report it to a trusted teacher and your parents.

Chapter 5
The Traitor

Let's face it, there's nothing worse than being betrayed by your friend. One minute she's your best bud, and the next she's dumped you for a new group of friends and acts like you don't exist. Or maybe she's flirting with your boyfriend. Or even worse, maybe she blabbed something about you that was supposed to be top secret. You thought you could trust her, but you're realizing now that you can't. You've just encountered the Traitor.

 NEW TEXT FROM CAROLE, 14: Having ur BFs treat u mean can really mess with ur self-esteem.

DEAR DR. ERIKA:

Nicole was always the flirtatious type. She was short, super skinny and had an ego that surpassed her small size. Getting all the attention in the room was her one goal, and I discovered to what great lengths she would go to get it.

She had been one of my very best friends for three years—we ran track together—when I told her I was interested in a shy boy, Chad, who indicated that he kinda liked me as well.

So right away Nicole and I organized a group date with Chad, Nicole, Ann, me, and several other good friends, guys and girls. But I could tell it was tearing Nicole up to see Chad giving me all his attention and not her. A true friend is supposed to be happy for you when you find a good guy to date, but not Nicole. She began flirting with him right in front of me. It was outrageous.

I am a shy person, as is Chad, so Nicole set out to prove she could be wilder and more outgoing than I am. I never had any classes with Chad, but when I would be walking down the hall with Nicole and my other friends and we'd pass him, Nicole's voice was always the loudest when saying hello: "Hi Chad! Hi Chad!!!"

When Chad and I started drifting apart, it took me a while to realize that Nicole was the cause. It all sunk in a few months later when Chad asked Nicole to the prom and not me. She would not even tell me herself that

Chad had asked her because she knew it would upset me so. After the prom, Nicole said Chad was a real bore, and that she didn't even like him, so why did she have to ruin things for me?

~Shelby, 16

DEAR DR. ERIKA:

All year long, my friend Janet has been talking about the big party her parents will give her when she turns sixteen. It's going to be a huge, huge event with lots of kids invited, including cute guys! We've been talking about it almost every day. I've helped her with most of the planning because even though she is super smart, Janet doesn't have the most creative ideas. So here we've been putting our heads together and making all the great plans—I spent hours coming up with songs she likes for the deejay to play! There's going to be a tent and a cookout and we made a list of games together. I even helped write out the invitations.

So the day before yesterday all the girls at school, well, quite a few, were showing off their invitations. It made me so happy. This was my work! When they said, "Did you get yours?" I had a sinking feeling but said, "Oh, the mail's slow at our house," but the invitation didn't come. And when I mentioned it to Janet, like maybe it got lost, she turned pink all over and said her mother said the guest list was way long and she had to cut it and you know. . . .

When I heard her go on and on, I felt my heart break into a million pieces.

~Lynda, 17

FYI

A traitor is someone who betrays a sacred trust. She misleads and deceives you, and not just in minor stuff, but in some major way. So being the victim of a traitor can really hurt.

A traitor is sneaky; a traitor is dishonest. She's so two-faced that she plays her part perfectly, and you never suspect anything. Why would you? After all, this girl is one of your best friends, and has been for years. You're so glad you have her to confide in and goof around with. Whew, the things you two can get into.

Meanwhile, she's also sharing with you what's going on with her, and talking frankly and holding nothing back. Maybe she's the one friend you rely on most. A true BFF. When something hits the fan, you can turn to her and just let it all out—whatever deep dark secrets you may harbor, even if it's something you're ashamed of, even the things you have never even admitted to yourself.

So yes, your friendship is sacred, at least to you. That's what makes the Traitor one of the worst of the mean chicks—and unfortunately she's not as easy to spot as some of the others.

Then one day you find out that everything you have revealed in confidence has been blabbed about everywhere,

even online. This is a hard thing to take. It's like a strong earthquake got you. It feels like your feelings have been totally trashed!

 NEW TEXT FROM PHOEBE, 15: When ur BFF turns on U and says mean things 2U—or about U—ugh, it's the worst! You can't really put it in words.

What a horrible wake-up call this is, to find out that who you thought was your best pal is really against you and never was truly for you to begin with. That kind of realization can really hurt you deeply.

UNIVERSAL HIGH SCHOOL

Lainie and Tonya have known each other all their lives and now attend the same high school. And yet suddenly something went wrong between them. Here's their story, according to Tonya:

Lainie's always been my best friend among all my friends and we've trusted each other completely. I've told her things I've never told anyone else: things that bother me, embarrassing stuff, everything.

One day Lainie began talking about this new guy she liked. I didn't even know who he was and figured Lainie and he wouldn't last very long because Lainie's "relationships" never did.

When I finally met the new guy, needless to say, I was not impressed. He was the total opposite of what she had always looked for in a boyfriend, and I wasn't the only one who didn't like him. None of our other friends did either, but we all tried to be nice for her sake, which wasn't easy.

He seemed jealous of my relationship with Lainie, and due to this, he was always taking jabs at me, cutting me down. I got used to it, but it still hurt, especially when I realized that Lainie ignored my pain. Her making excuses for or ignoring his digs at me was agonizing, and at times almost brought me to tears. Then everything really hit the fan.

While I spent the night at her house, Lainie called the guy at midnight to chat. I guess her thumbs got tired of texting. Anyway, I got bored and fell asleep. When my mom asked me later about the night, I said, not thinking, "I fell asleep while Lainie was still talking on the phone."

That simple statement caused all sorts of trouble. My mother repeated it to Lainie's parents, who were suspicious of the new guy to begin with, and they ran with what I had said.

That Monday at school, Lainie confronted me. I told her I was innocent because I had never told anyone she was talking to her boyfriend at midnight. I just said she was on the phone! And I was very disappointed that she didn't have enough faith in me to believe that I would never tell anyone about her talking to him so late.

To avoid making her even madder, I decided to keep my distance from Lainie for a while. Instead of realizing that I was trying to give her time to cool off, she saw this as clear proof of my guilt.

There were several more confrontations: Lainie wouldn't give because she believed it was my fault; I wouldn't give because I felt I was innocent in the whole matter. But what was the worst, Lainie told her side to everyone in our group, so they all turned against me. I'd done nothing, and yet they acted as if it was my fault. Even worse, she blabbed about all my secrets. This upset me so much I could hardly keep going, and it lasted until the school year was over. By then Lainie's relationship with the new guy was way ancient history. Now we're good friends again, sorta anyway. However, to this day, I can't get over the fact that Lainie ever thought I'd betrayed her. She betrayed me! And that's a fact!

So you see how sometimes even the best of friends can suddenly start acting like traitors, so you've got to guard yourself against this type of behavior! Here's a way to find out if you're vulnerable to the kind of betrayal we're talking about.

FAST QUIZ

Traitors Among Us—Beware!

1. You have been assigned a major project that requires interviewing older people about World War II. You and your best bud spend hours formulating your questions and discussing how you will record the answers and how to videotape the participants. You're so psyched about this assignment, which will be the major grade for this semester. When you're ready to start, your best friend says she's decided to work with another girl. You:

A. Hide your hurt feelings and tell her it's okay. If she steals your ideas and gets a better grade than you there's nothing you can do about it now. Besides, you've never been one to stand out in the crowd. A B is almost as good as an A, and a C isn't bad, either.

B. Drop your project entirely and ask if you can join in their group. You let them use all of your top ideas and research, and add it to their own, even though they don't seem very appreciative. It's better than working by yourself, and besides, there's not as much work to do with several of you splitting the responsibilities.

C. You're really ticked off that she bailed on you, but you fight fire with fire. You add up all the hours you already put into this project and tell your "best" friend she better give you major credit in her report, or she can't use the information at all. Plus, you make sure to spread it around your group of friends that she totally ditched you. If you get them all on your side then she'll feel extra guilty about skipping out. Two can play at this game!

D. Your feelings are hurt, but you pair up with another girl who doesn't have a partner and do the best work ever in your life. You pour yourself into the project. Once you've had the chance to stop steaming at her, write your friend an e-mail or give her a call after school and tell her how you feel. If she's a true friend, she'll listen and understand, and maybe the two of you can work it out. If she gets all defensive, maybe it's time to realize that your best bud doesn't have the best intentions.

2. You're trying out for the Junior Follies—the annual student talent show at your school. For weeks, you and your best friend have been rehearsing a routine for your fave song. The plan is that you will sing and your best friend will dance. She's been taking ballet lessons for eons. But on the day of dress rehearsal, your friend totally changes her tune and decides she wants to dance alone to a recorded version of the song. You:

A. Drop out of the show. What's the use—it will be sooo embarrassing when two different acts use the same song. And there's no way you can get up on that stage all by yourself! Besides, she's a better dancer than you are a singer, anyway. Why not let her have the spotlight?

B. Beg and plead for her to stay with you for the act. You promise her you'll buy her tickets to the next Taylor Swift concert, let her borrow your fave sweater that you never let her lay a hand on— anything. If that fails, you tell on her to the faculty sponsor and make her perform with you. Whatever it takes to avoid being on that stage alone in front of the whole school!

C. Cause a scene that would make even the snottiest prima donna shake in her shoes. You remind her that she wouldn't even have a routine without you since the whole thing was your idea in the first place! You stomp around, tell everyone what a traitor she is, and scream until you're hoarse. That way you'll lose your singing voice and you can lay double blame on her when you have to quit the show.

D. Take a little time to get over the shock, then recoup and regroup. Maybe it's better this way. You know you'll give it your best shot; you'll just get out there and sing like Charlotte Church. Who knows, there may even be a couple of record company scouts in the audience. Hey, you could be the next *American Idol!*

3. It's prom time, and you and your best friend are totally dateless. The guys you're interested in all have girlfriends, and the dudes who're interested in you are duds. No prob—you decide that you'll go by yourselves and have a blast anyway. You'll be the divas of the dance with your awesome 'dos and sexy shoes. And you won't have to worry about impressing some dumb guy. One hour before the prom, your friend calls to tell you she has a date! With Clyde, the most pitiful perv in the whole school. Nobody likes him, not because of his looks or nerd quotient, but because he takes pictures of, um, "himself," and texts the pics to girls and always tries to look down girls' shirts! You:

A. Stay in your room with a pint of cookie dough ice cream and DVDs of *Glee.* A dynamic duo would have been totally cool, but you can't believe you got dumped for Creepy Clyde. Well, it would be too embarrassing to show up all alone. Better luck next year!

B. Rush excitedly over to your friend's house, help fix her hair and makeup, and make sure to bring your dress with you. With any luck, she can fix you up with one of Clyde's buddies. Hey, it may not be your dream date, but it's better than staying home.

C. Call Clyde and tell him every nasty thing your friend has ever said about him! You even manage to come up with a few more of your own, and you're quite proud of your creativity. You warn him to stay away from your friend, or you'll turn him in for carrying around porno mags. If you're dateless for the prom, you'll make sure your friend will be, too!

D. Go to the prom dressed to kill, boogie down all night long, and have a blast. Your friend is on her own trip, but you don't need a guy to have fun. These days, flying solo is just as hip as doing the date thing. Meanwhile, you spot your bud in the corner, trying to keep Clyde from breathing down her neck. You'll give her a call later to get the dish and to comfort her, but you're not going to let her decision bring you down.

4. A special guy you've admired from way back sends you an e-mail that's sweet and touching. It's all about how he's been noticing you, too, and wants to talk to you tomorrow after second period. You're freaking out with joy and forward this e-mail to your best friend, making sure to label it "TOP SECRET!!!!" Your hopes for romance are crushed when you discover, to your horror, that she's forwarded it to the whole class! You:

A. Feel like dropping out of school—right this sec. You'd rather die than face your crush, and you definitely can't face your classmates tomorrow. But maybe if you're late to first period and have your mom dismiss you early, you can ignore them and they'll forget about it. As far as your ex "best" friend goes, you're too hurt to face her, so you just lay low until the whole thing blows over. Or until you graduate.

B. See your friend in the hallway and pretend as though nothing has happened. After all, if you're ticked off at her you won't have anyone to sit with at lunch or to hang out with this weekend. So she made a mistake. When you see your crush in the hall, you avoid his gaze and act like you don't even know him. It's better than dealing with the humiliation of having your feelings exposed. There are plenty of other fish in the sea, right?

C. Immediately set up a fake Facebook page for your friend, detailing all of her deepest and most personal issues. As the coup de grace, you decorate the wall with that awful picture of her right after she got her wisdom teeth out that you swore you'd never show to anyone. Then you forward the link to everyone in your class. You are a girl of the cyber world, and you fight fire with fire!

D. Are totally embarrassed—and furious. After you've cooled down a little, you have a long talk with your friend. You tell her how much she's hurt you and that she's broken your trust. You also let her know that you won't put up with this type of thing very long before you tell her to hit the road. As for your crush, well, it's not exactly a great storybook romance, but since he knows how you feel anyway, you might as well act on it. Of course, you tell him how this happened and apologize. Then wait. You never know where this could lead!

Now it's time to find out how you did. Total up your answers.

ANSWERS

If you answered mostly As: Pick your head up, girl! Haven't you learned by now that running away from your problems will never solve them? Next time, just deal with it. Let the Traitor know that she hurt you and that you're not going to put up with it. If telling her face to face isn't your thing, maybe you can e-mail her and let her know how you feel. If you want to make good friends you've got to be a good friend, and part of being a good friend is being able to talk about how you feel. If you don't take a stand for yourself, your friends are going to keep walking all over you. Don't be discouraged, though. Knowledge is power, so take the power you get from this book and hold your head up high!

If you answered mostly Bs: Why do you keep clinging to this friend when she treats you like an enemy? You owe yourself more than hanging around with a dishonest friend and making yourself miserable. You deserve better than that, and there are plenty of girls to hang around with. You're a cool chick, not a doormat. Try giving some other girls a chance and see what it's like to have real friends, not passing trends!

If you answered mostly Cs: What are you trying to gain from getting back at your formerly "best" friend? What's done is done, so turning into a mean queen yourself isn't going to help a bit. Sure, she broke your trust, and that really hurts. Standing up for yourself is definitely a plus, but waging a war of revenge isn't the way to win—that only makes you a loser in the end. You're strong, smart, and sweet, and you want to stay that way. Playing these games will only make you sour.

If you answered mostly Ds: What a girl! You let yourself feel the pain that always comes when someone you care about betrays you. And you face up to the Traitor! But then you don't wallow in your misery for long because you know there are so many great chicks out there, and it won't be long until you will find one that's a true friend, not a jealous weasel. So forge new friendships—with both girls and guys. The world is your oyster; it's up to you to find the pearls.

If you have a mixture of As, Bs, Cs, and Ds: Review all of the above. Obviously, there's a little bit of every-thing in you, which is great. Now, can you work on having a little more of that Answer-D attitude?

TRAITOR SMARTS—WHAT SHOULD YOU KNOW ABOUT THE TRAITOR?

A one-time occurrence of betrayal can be bad enough, but what if you just found out that your best bud has been betraying you for months? What you need to know:

★ The Traitor has most likely been betrayed herself in the past, but rather than learn from this bad experience and become an especially good friend, she has become an imitator of treacherous behavior.

★ She doesn't know the true meaning of friendship. Therefore, the Traitor breaks a trust as easily as she'd snap a twig. If you still hang out with her, proceed with extreme caution!

★ Whatever problems she's had in the past, don't excuse the Traitor's behavior. Once she's betrayed you, stay away from her for as long as you wish. Maybe slowly and over time trust can be rebuilt, but don't feel any pressure. Think about the Traitor long and hard, and then you decide if you want to give her another chance.

RAPID RESPONSE: WHAT YOU SHOULD DO ABOUT THE TRAITOR

Want some top tips when faced with the Traitor?

Know that traitors don't come with a warning sign; they often present themselves like real nice girls. Yet no matter what you may think at the time, you can and will get over being hurt by a friend. It may take a while, but everything worthwhile does, and rebuilding trust after you've cleared the air isn't easy. But it will benefit you—you'll emerge from this stronger and better and smarter. And you may even be able to teach the Traitor how great a real friend can be!

Whatever you do, don't get cynical and bitter and turn your back on other girls forever. There are real friends out there, who will be loyal to you no matter what. Don't start doubting that there can be real friends, like Allie did after her longtime best friend suddenly revealed her true colors.

You have one new e-mail: After all the years we put into our friendship, it was when I got first chair in band and my best friend didn't that showed how she really felt about me. So our being buds was never built on anything lasting. Makes you wonder: Is there no real friendship? Is it all fake? ~Allie, 14

Real friendships take years to build, and it's up to you to use good judgment in choosing your friends. But time alone isn't the only way to measure the strength of a friendship.

WHAT I WENT THROUGH—A REAL-LIFE STORY FROM BUFFY, 18

Leigh and I have been friends for a long, long time. We live in the same neighborhood and officially met at the beginning of middle school. Ever since, we started the tradition of always going holiday shopping together at the mall. We picked the

first Saturday in December as the day and discussed it all year
long. Many of our other friends would join us when they
could, but the two of us never missed our yearly routine.

It would always be exactly the same: First, we walked to
the center where the little kids had their picture taken with
Santa Claus sitting on a bench in
front of a giant gingerbread house.
We'd spend half an hour or so
watching them and laughing over the
cute kids and reminiscing about the
time when we were little kids ourselves. Then we'd amble over to the
food court for lunch. It was always
veggie pizza and chocolate ice cream with
sprinkles. And then, lists in hand, we'd hit the stores
hard and spend all our carefully saved cash.

This year, our senior year, Leigh changed schools. At first
that was okay, but then we started not to talk and spend as
much time together anymore. We used to talk and see each
other every day, but now we were lucky if we did this three
times a week. Of course, we still texted and tweeted like crazy.

Anyway, December was coming up. I'd been hoarding
all the extra money I made baby-sitting, and I knew Leigh
was doing exactly the same. This year, we'd be able to buy
really nice gifts. Plus, a few new stores we were really
excited to try were opening just in time for the holidays.

Excitedly, I called Leigh a week before the day and
asked her if she was planning to drive or should I. Well, did
I get a surprise. Leigh said she was going on a family trip
and would be out of town.

✉ **You have one new e-mail:** Always try to have more than one friend. If something was to happen in one relationship, it's important that a girl has other pals to turn to. So don't ever shut yourself off. No girl is an island, you know? ~Tangela, 16

I was shocked because that had never ever happened before, but I understood. I decided to go to the mall anyway with several other girls because the routine had become so drilled into my head. Guess the same thing had happened to Leigh, because when I got to the gingerbread house, there she was laughing and joking with some new friends.

It turned out she had lied to me: There was no family trip planned. But why couldn't she just have told me the truth? Now we still talk some, we're still friends—sorta— but it's always like there's a dark cloud hanging over us.

Dr. Erika's Response

Sure, Buffy feels betrayed, but that's because she's never cleared the air. The cloud of Leigh's lie is still hanging over their friendship. But if Buffy wants to keep Leigh as a life-long friend and wants to reclaim the real close friendship they used to have, some housecleaning is called for. That should start with a heart-to-heart talk.

DEAR DIARY

Have you ever been betrayed or been turned against by a best friend? Was it someone you trusted with your deepest secrets? Whom you loaned money to, shared your lunch with, and even swapped clothes with?

If you have, write about it in your diary. Be sure to put in every thought that crossed your mind, every reaction, every feeling you had or still have. How did it make you feel to realize that your "friend" was just using you? Don't worry about how it sounds or if it doesn't make any sense; just get it all out. Maybe you're better at poetry. If so, then write a poem or dash off a song. Whatever helps you get through your feelings, write it out. This is no one's business but your own.

You have one new e-mail: Finding loyal true friends that last can be way tough. But don't give up. One of my supposed best friends was always plotting behind the scenes to keep me from making new friends. She wanted me to have nobody. But once I found out the truth, I felt sorry for her and was able to move on. ~Patty Ann, 17

Next, make a list of all of the words that describe what your friend did. Look at the list closely. Next to each negative word, write down a positive word or sentence that turns things around, like "tell the truth," "be up front," "admit your mistake," "apologize," and so on. Look at this list even more closely, and make a promise to yourself that you'll put it to good use. These words are the way you'll treat all of your friends from now on.

FAB FIXES FOR WHATEVER ATTITUDE AILS YOU

Growing up is a time of ups and downs, a real roller coaster of emotions. One moment you're on top of the world; the next you feel lower than an ant. Remember, it's normal to have fleeting feelings of inferiority. Also, sometimes you'll find yourself having negative feelings about other girls, too, even those who have never been mean to you. Suddenly, you're envious of some of them or wish they wouldn't win the tennis match, the student council election, or first place at the science fair.

But that's all part of growing into the wonderful person you're meant to be. Feeling conflicting emotions about yourself and your best pals is normal. Even the fact that you cover up any spiteful thoughts and congratulate your friends insincerely is normal, too.

You see, your emotional well-being is just growing along with the rest of you, and growth isn't always smooth and straightforward. There are a few detours ahead for everyone, even a roundabout or two. Still, should you come down with a serious case of fraud-itude, when you suddenly find yourself feeling jealous of your best friends and wishing bad things on them, and yet you act so fakey nice, try using some of the tips below.

Rx: Fighting Fraud-itude

Once a day:

1. Dismiss any unfriendly thoughts at once—swat them away—and replace them with positive, encouraging

ones. For example, instead of thinking, "I want Cara to come in second," say out loud, "I hope Cara will get first place!" Fight the "green monster" of envy and you'll feel like you're on top of the world!

2. We all need an outlet for our mean or envious thoughts sometimes, but that doesn't mean we should take them out on our friends. Write them down in your diary instead to get them out of your system. Then forget all about them. You'll see—just writing them down often erases them from your mind.

3. If a friend of yours points out that you've recently been acting like a witch, don't get all huffy; take this as an opportunity to improve your character. Your friend wouldn't point out this flaw in you if she didn't care. Similarly, if it's you who's been treated treacherously, be as forgiving as you can. Try to give a real good friend another chance, but only if you feel you can. When dealing with Traitors, your gut instinct will always be your best guide.

THE BOTTOM LINE

So, here's the bottom line on Traitors:

★ The girl world can be tough, but remember, there are all kinds of great chicks out there just waiting to be your friends. Be resilient! By learning to bounce back from a bad situation or a betrayal, you're empowering yourself. Practice snapping back and feeling more in control—because you are.

★ On the road to success (or maybe to graduation), try to think of betrayal as another lesson to be learned, not a permanent scar that you must carry with you. Life will be full of stumbling blocks— it's up to you whether you want to avoid them or overcome them or use them as building material for your best future. Sure, it's great to have friends that you trust, but beware of confiding too early on in a friendship. Take it easy; take it slow. Good friendships take a while to grow!

★ Know that friends can make mistakes, no matter how close you may be. Okay, so maybe your friend acted like a total jerk. But deep down, if you know she's a great chick, full of fun times and great laughs and long talks and you never know what hilarious stuff she'll text next, consider giving her another chance. To find out if your friendship is worth saving, have a serious talk with the Traitor. If she apologizes and says she's really sorry, that's a good sign. After a long talk and some fence mending, your friendship could become stronger than before.

Chapter 6
The Clique Chick

WHAT MAKES THE CLIQUE CHICK TICK?

Watch out for this girl—she can be the most dangerous of all because she's a double—even triple—threat. She may be a Snob, Gossip, Teaser, Bully, or a Traitor—but her true colors come out only when she's surrounded by her group. When she's alone she's not so bad, but when she's with her clique it's a brand-new ball game. That's why some girls are more afraid of this type of girl than of any other.

 NEW TEXT FROM JOSIE, 15: Girls tease other girls b/c they don't like who u are or because ur not in their clique. So they try 2 get u2b just like them and do things u shouldn't. What can u do when the most popular girl expects u 2 do it?

You can do a lot to counteract the effects of those in a clique. Just because the most popular girl in school (and her gal pals) expects you to do something you know isn't right, you don't have to bite. So what's her deal, anyway? What's behind the Clique Chick? Let's find out.

DEAR DR. ERIKA,

One of the girls in my class gets everything—every award, every honor, every time she's the one nominated for whatever. It makes me so sick. When there's a vote, I don't even participate anymore, because she gets it anyway. No need to nominate or campaign or even try to go out for anything I'm interested in. She gets the nomination, she is named homecoming representative, she has her picture and is quoted in the school paper. It's as if she speaks for the whole class.

~Lyssa, 15

DEAR DR. ERIKA:

I'm not a nerd or anything but not slutty either, and lately whenever I go to parties, people are getting into stuff like beer and cigarettes, you know. Well, I don't want to drink or smoke or do worse stuff. But just last weekend I actually considered picking up a beer just to fit in. The only thing that stopped me was this girl's parents showing up.

~Elise, 16

FYI

A Clique Chick is a girl who doesn't make a move without her entourage. That's her train of followers and gal pals. Some of them might even be part of very tight cliques that formed way back in kindergarten or grade school.

These cliques can consist of one or even several dozen girls, but what they all have in common is that they cluster around a girl who's Miss Popularity because of her looks or the way she acts or maybe her material possessions. From elementary school on, the Clique Chick isn't too concerned about grades or sports. Mostly, she's concerned about herself—her looks, her clothes, her hair, all of her expensive possessions. At least that's the way it seems from the outside. But there's no doubt about one thing: The Clique Chick cares about having many, many friends—both online and in life.

To rule over her many gal pals, the Clique Chick spends serious time in front of the mirror worrying about what to wear, how to fix her bangs, how not to gain weight. She's almost always high maintenance. She may have her nails done professionally, her hair high or low lighted, and stress out over her prom dress far in advance, sometimes years ahead of the actual event.

Super Clique Chicks always have a loyal following. From early on, they spend most of their free time talking to and advising other girls, who're desperately trying to become more like the top chick. They talk about who likes whom, who will ask whom for a date, and who should get invited to the next party. It's often a he said/she said chit-chat, with the betas followers reporting to the alpha top chick what's being said.

Any true Clique Chick is the center of many other girls' attention, and naturally, she can be harsh in dealing with the members of her clique and other girls. She can decree who's in and who's out, what's perfect and what's passé, and there's no appealing her decision. What's being said about others isn't important.

Cliques are the gatherings of girls who can't yet stand on their own two feet. For them, there's safety in numbers. It's like a fab family, especially for girls who feel unloved at home or think no one cares. And the top Clique Chick comes from a similar home situation. Maybe she's an only child with super busy parents who have their attention elsewhere. Or she comes from a background that's not demonstrative and doesn't show warmth, so the clique queen has to get it from her court—all the adulation and admiration she feels she deserves but has been deprived of.

And whatever the alpha chick's age, she has picked up adult characteristics prematurely. She's a pseudo grownup on the one hand; on the other, she's way immature. She wants a sisterhood swarming around her to make up for the attention she lacks. Even though she had to grow up fast, she has a childlike value system. She thinks clothes, nails, hair, and purses are what life's all about. And yet deep down, she's loving and caring, but also trying so hard to make up for what's missing, that she often turns even her own mom, sisters, and aunts into her entourage. Her frequent Barbie-doll appearance reinforces her status. So, overall, a Clique Chick is a girl who has alpha status and can—at times—be extremely mean, rude, cold, or cutting. In other words, a real pain in the asterisk.

WHAT HAPPENED AT THE PROM—A REAL-LIFE STORY AS TOLD BY A TEACHER

The two girls swept into the immaculately decorated gym by different doors. Both were accompanied by their boy-friend du jour and several other less-popular couples. As they advanced toward each other, a huge pall fell over the lively party. Prior to that moment, at least 500 kids and numerous teachers and parent chaperones had been dancing, drinking punch, and talking animatedly about which girl would be named prom queen that night.

Now a palpable gloom brought everything, even the expensive band, to a screeching halt. Why?

Because these two super Clique Chicks were wearing the same elaborate designer prom dress in the same vivid color—aquamarine. Plus, their long blond hair was coifed in the exact same elegant up-do. What was even worse: Even their nails and eye shadow—a frosty pale blue—was the same, as were their 3" spaghetti-strap silver sandals.

What a total disaster. Only their wrist corsages were different, but not much. One was fashioned of white-blue orchids matching the nail polish and eye shadow. The other was made of white-silver orchids matching the sandals.

And then what happened? The Clique Chicks stopped five feet from each other and stared. And glared. In total silence.

Finally, the festivities started again, tentatively at first. The band picked up, the other kids started moving again, but everyone's head craned as they kept looking at the "twins." That meant the party began to drag. It was like a layer of molasses had been poured on the shiny dance floor, making the dancers slog along, while their mouths were at a fevered pitch, verbally taking sides with their favorite twin. It was like a standoff in a bad Western movie, with the two factions daring each other to make the first move. And how the camera phones click-clicked.

Soon, here and there threats began to rise like wisps of smoke. Some of the other girls started heading for the punch bowl vowing to be the first to "accidentally" throw a cup of punch on their "enemy's" gown, while some of the boys were starting to vent their anger on the enemy's innocent date.

In order to prevent any fights from breaking out, the prom had to be closed down and everyone went home. But neither the girls nor anyone else present ever forgot the "Prom That Wasn't." How could they?

Dr. Erika's Response

The prom goers folded without giving it a good try. All of them should have sent the jealous chicks and their chums packing, cleaned house so to speak, and then had the social event of the century. Another solution might have been to tell the girls just to shake it off.

But instead, the teachers and chaperones overreacted, but who can blame them? They were afraid that after the unfortunate occurrence, the prom wouldn't have worked. And the longer the competing twin queens were in the same room, their eyes shooting hateful arrows at one another, the closer the situation came to getting out of hand. While there wasn't much chance of the top Clique Chicks getting into a fist fight, their entourage was on the verge of trading licks. And in order to prevent that, the prom was cancelled. But it was a wimpy way out—why did the innocent bystanders have to get punished too? Think of all the time and money they had invested in this gala event, only to have two super-mean Clique Chicks jealously ruin everything for everyone.

CLIQUE LIT?

Isn't it a real shame that so many other kids missed out on their prom because of two girls? You can help put a stop to this type of behavior by empowering yourself against Clique Chicks. So ask yourself: Are you susceptible to any Clique Chick tricks? Let's take a quiz and find out.

FAST QUIZ

Are You a Clique Chick?

1. Senior Skip Day has long been a tradition at your school. Only one problem—you're not a senior yet! Still, the alpha girl in your grade and all her attendants and friends have decided to observe Skip Day, too, this year. You:

    A. Make sure you sneeze and cough several times during class before the Skip Day so you can "legitimately" stay home nursing your li'l 'ole cold and won't have to be out in the cruel world. Better to hide than have to decide where you stand on ditching class.

    B. Go wherever the wind blows you. If you have a class with some people who are skipping, you talk as if you're going to skip, too. If you run into a group of friends who thinks skipping is dumb, you agree with them.

C. Don't let the Clique Chick dictate when you cut class. Just who does she think she is, anyway? You tell her she's totally unoriginal for skipping on Senior Skip Day. Everyone will know what she's up to, anyway. When you feel like skipping school, you'll skip school, but on her orders? Not on your life!

D. Know what you want in life—major success!—and the prerequisite for that is doing your best in school. Sure, sleeping late and lounging around the house all day is tempting, but you've got a lot to do. Besides, your parents can be super cool about that kind of stuff. In fact, your mom promised you a free day of shopping and movies if you bring your history grade up, and you're saving your skip day for that!

2. On a field trip to the nearby university with your advanced biology class, your teacher tells you to carefully check out the world-famous marine lab, then meet for lunch at the student union. The Clique Chick decides that the group should skip the lab and opts instead for a way long lunch. You:

A. Hurry to the bathroom in the marine lab lobby, where you hop on the throne and peruse a pamphlet on the exhibits. That way you're okay with both the clique and the teacher. Aren't you smart!

B. Volunteer to swear to the teacher that you saw the clique in the exhibit hall with your very own eyes.

That means you have to personally stroll through that lame place, but anything to get an in with the ins! You're *there*. Next big venture, you won't have to be a "bencher" anymore.

C. Skip the morning lab plus the afternoon junk—a lecture on the Jacques Cousteau Institute—as well, and hang out with a couple of hot college guys. And if that Barbie-doll diva or any of her devotees opens her trap, you'll spill it about what they were doing all afternoon.

D. Check out the exhibit. Let the Clique Chick and her crew play their baby games, you've got no use for them. Hey, marine biology stuff may not be your bag, but at least it's a day out of school. Besides, even though English lit is more your style, some of it's interesting, anyway. Might as well scope it out while you're here.

3. At the end-of-the-year class picnic, everyone's participating in silly games—such as the three-legged sack race, the water-balloon fight, the rope pulling, and the egg toss—for which points are allotted to the participants. You and your group are desperately trying to win the huge trophy, and you do! Afterward, when you and the rest of your friends look over the tally sheet, you notice that somebody made a mistake in adding up the scores. You and your clique actually came in second. Ouch! You:

A. Inch away and make sure to help clean up the picnic grounds. Score keeping isn't your responsibility, so why fret?

B. You just happen to have a pen in the exact color of the one used on the tally sheet and offer to make an 8 out of the 3. No one will even notice, your team will win, and you'll be the cool chick of the day!

C. Spend the rest of the afternoon proudly showing off "your" trophy, loudly saying that the other teams looked like they were trying out to be pro wrestlers. Too bad for them!

D. Recheck the scores slowly, then—no matter how much you hate doing it—show the mistake to your teammates, then take it to the picnic supervisors. Let them handle the problem. It's such a bummer you have to give the trophy back, but your team had a blast in the competitions, anyway. Despite your stripped gold medal and some slightly wounded egos, you manage to rally the girls together for ice cream sundaes—a soul soother if ever there was one!

4. When the yearbooks come out, you and your group have an autograph session and discuss what's going to be different in next year's annual. The leader in your group suggests that the senior superlative section needs help. Besides the usual categories, she suggests your class should start a new trend and vote for Worst Dressed, Worst Grades, Worst Athletes, Ugliest, and so on. Everybody just loves the idea—what a riot!—and they start tossing around the names of classmates that were just born for the new categories. You:

A. Cringe in fear, hoping and praying that nobody mentions your name in connection with any of the new superlatives! Okay, so not everyone can be on top of her fashion game, but is that any reason to be labeled for all eternity as a loser?

B. Hustle to act as super secretary, taking stellar notes and joining in enthusiastically. By being an active participant, you're hoping to score major bonus points with the leader of the group and your faculty sponsor. And best of all, insiders can't be nominated! So what if a few total losers get labeled in the process? As long as it's not you, you're fine with whatever the group wants.

C. Think it's a horrible idea, and you speak your mind. You're usually not out to label anyone, but just to even the score, you suggest to the leader of the clique that you just thought of two categories she'd be perfect for—Most Shallow and Tackiest Attitude. And then you take a paper poll of the whole student body—with her name listed under those categories: "Check if you agree." You don't mind polling yourself several times to prove your point. Ballot stuffing is okay when it's for the right reason, isn't it?

D. Feel uncomfortable with the new nasty superlatives, and you let the group know about it. The purpose of the yearbook is to remind your class of good memories, not bad or degrading ones. Who wants to be remembered by a class that would vote for such rude categories, anyway? As an alternative, you suggest a new section of funny superlatives for some of the most popular teachers just to lighten things up a bit.

Now it's time to find out how you did. Total up your answers.

ANSWERS

If you answered mostly As: You may not be the alpha chick in your group, but you're definitely guilty of being a chicklet. When are you going to realize that your opinions mean something and that expressing them is powerful? There's nothing in the girl world that you can't handle. Just take a deep breath and face your fear factor. Stand up to those other girls! You deserve better than living in their shadows, and it's time you did the right thing for you.

If you answered mostly Bs: You're so anxious to gain attention and be part of the group that you sacrifice yourself to be part of the popular chick landscape. Next time, stop and think before you rush to cater to the whims of the Clique Chick and her crew. Why are you doing this? Do you really need their approval that badly? Here's a tip: Try pleasing yourself for a change, rather than trying so hard to please others. The world is at your fingertips; all you have to do is reach out and grab it.

If you answered mostly Cs: The good news is that you're an energetic action girl. While your intentions may start off on the right foot, the bad news is that you may be misapplying your energy, and in loose-cannon style. Expressing your opinion is great, but as they say, "Timing is everything." Next time, give your brain a chance to shift into high gear before you spring into action. If you do that, you're almost sure to gain the respect of your classmates. You are a smart girl, and you have lots of good things to offer the girl world. But first things first—get a grip on that lip! You may be hurting others when you're only trying to help.

If you answered mostly Ds: You have good self-esteem and know how to handle yourself when confronted with Clique Chicks with mean tricks up their sleeve. One of those mean tricks is to try to get you to fold under pressure—peer pressure that is. But you're not folding; you are holding on to your good values. And by your great example, even some other girls can learn to be strong.

If you have a mixture of As, Bs, Cs, and Ds: Review all of the above. Obviously, there's a little bit of everything in you, which is great. Now can you work on having a little more of that D attitude?

 NEW TEXT FROM JEWEL, 14: If all the girls in our school would get together in one caring clique, just think of how much we could get done.

CLIQUE CHICK SMARTS—WHAT SHOULD YOU KNOW ABOUT THE CLIQUE CHICK?

Here's a list of things to keep in mind about the Clique Chick:

★ Know that mean clique conduct often involves putting the clique squeeze, otherwise known as peer pressure, on you. Peer pressure can bring out either the best or the worst in you. All you have to do is examine it and ask yourself what your peers are really pressuring you to do.

★ At first, clique squeeze might seem pretty harmless, like how you dress or wear your hair. While part of finding yourself can mean going along with the pack, be sure to watch your back around this type of behavior. First, it may only be clothes or hair, but that can expand into other things, like who you can and can't date, or even being cruel to other girls. Don't get caught up in that type of mean game. Keep yourself safe, and always be true to your goals and your soul.

★ So focus on yourself, your talents, and your potential. Rather than spending your energy on trying to please the alphas or betas, be the strong gamma independent mind you are and do what enhances your own life and what contributes to your fabulous future. You're on your way to growth and greatness.

RAPID RESPONSE: WHAT YOU SHOULD DO ABOUT THE CLIQUE CHICK

Follow these steps to guard against the Clique Chicks:

1. Fight the clique squeeze at your school by giving the ruling clique of chicks at your school the cold shoulder. Be independent-minded and develop your own style.

2. Stop worrying about what other girls want you to do and just be yourself. Did you know that *popular* actually means "average or ordinary"? Don't strive so hard to be just ordinary. Be extraordinary. Be outstanding! Be what you're meant to be—the best you can be.

3. Try sharing some of these tricks on dealing with cliques with other girls—maybe your little sister and her friends or even girls in grades lower than you. Tell a teacher that you and your friends want to volunteer, and talk to younger girls and help them survive and thrive in the girl world. By teaching others how to be strong, you are allowing your own strength to grow.

FAB FIXES FOR WHATEVER ATTITUDE AILS YOU

Now more so than ever, fashion plays a key role in our society. Just look at TV, magazines, pop-up and banner ads, and billboards—it's practically all you see! Every time you turn around, fashions can change from way wow to way yuck in a matter of weeks.

Naturally, it's fun to get together with your girls and talk fashion. But, unless you're a Paris Hilton, it's nearly impossible to keep up with every fancy fad. Think about it—trying out tons of new things can be super fun. It helps you learn about what you like and don't like. In other words, it helps you learn more about you. Whether the fad you're trying on is fashion or music or lifestyle, you're always learning, right? But in your quest for the best, what if you get too caught up in the latest and the greatest and forget about the you that's really inside, the true you? Sure, your new shoes match your new purse and they're totally hot! But what happens when your fashion attitude becomes Fad-itude?

Rx: Facing Up to Fad-itude

Just keep the following in mind:

1. Know that fads are great fun if they're not overdone. If it's in your budget, looks great on you, and your mom approves, then it's the thing to do. So go ahead and get that cute headband or some new glittery nail polish.

2. Fads can be fab, but don't follow them blindly. Pick and choose what to try and what to buy. And make sure that whatever you choose makes a statement about you—who you are and who you want to be. One of the greatest things about fashion is individuality; don't lose yours just to keep up with the race. Develop your fashion conviction, not an addiction.

3. With so much to worry about, it's easy to forget about reality. Next time you go crazy because you just have to have that new pair of jeans and nothing

else will do, give yourself a reality check, girl! No matter what fad you're following this week, don't forget to give to others. What about all those clothes you don't wear anymore? Instead of letting them take up room in your closet, why not donate them to a local clothing drive or Salvation Army store? Doing good deeds for others can be just as fun as doing good deeds for yourself, at times even more so.

So, enjoy yourself as you predict the next big fashion forecast, but remember, always be grateful, always be gracious. When it's all said and done, do you want someone to remember you for what you wore or for what gifts you gave to the world?

THE BOTTOM LINE

So, what's the bottom line on Clique Chicks and their fad-itudes? Read on:

★ Fads don't last; they fade fast. So next time you feel yourself getting caught up in a fad, step back. You're in charge—do what you want, be whom you like— just make sure you're being true to yourself.

★ Before getting involved with any group or clique, be sure to ask yourself, "What makes this clique tick? And what is the top chick really like?" If it's a crew getting together for friendship and fun or for scholarships or a worthy cause, embrace it. But if it's all for fakiness and show, step back and think a minute before you make that swan dive. Remember, popular means ordinary, not extraordinary. You are special, not unspecial.

★ If a certain mean chick and her clique are getting you down, then you can get out. Who needs to be around a leader who's a loser? You're growing, and becoming more "you" each and every day. Don't let any Clique Chick stand in the way of how smart, original, funny, and full of possibilities you really are.

Chapter 7
The Cyber Frenemy

You envy her being dropped off by a car from her mom's company every morning. She grabs her Michael Kors bag that matches her chunky disk earrings and sprints into the front lobby of the school. The crowds part automatically to make room for her. She glances at the gaggle of girls that moves toward her and hands one of them her purse, so she can dig out whatever electronic gadget in there has started beeping. Out of breath, she comes up with a BlackBerry, a Kindle, an iPod, and two iPhones, one her personal one, the other from her mom's work, both of which are chirping. Then she focuses on the individual members of the group and smiles: "Hey, guys."

As all of you say hey back, her eyes are like lasers. They scan everybody up and down critically. Before she's even finished, her thumbs start tapping out a message to everyone. You don't know if it's about a new rumor or about what some girl is wearing or her straggly hair.

Suddenly, she singles you out with her eagle eyes and her thumbs rev up into overdrive. You want to run and hide so bad. You don't want to be the next target of the Cyber Frenemy.

DEAR DR. ERIKA:

At lunch, we all go outside to the picnic benches. As soon we park ourselves, everyone whips out their cell phones. Then texting starts up, even though we're sitting right here and could just as well chat—using our vocal chords. Since I don't have a cell phone right now, I always sit there like a pumpkin on Easter—way out of place and totally overlooked, even kinda pitied. And when the bell rings, they dash off laughing about their digital messages and I'm left out—in the friggin' frigid cold.

~Juliana, 15

DEAR DR. ERIKA (VIA E-MAIL):

This one girl who's way popular posts a lot of cute pics on her Facebook page. But I'm always cropped out! It's like I'm not even there. I really feel like I belong to the enemy camp.

~Leigha, 16

FYI

The lesser of the mean cyber-chick types is the Cyber Frenemy. This is a girl who either used to be your friend or still is your friend, but isn't on board as a 100 percent bud. She's more like a 60/40 friend. Sometimes she can even be a 40/60 or 25/75 friend, meaning more times than not, she's not so hot as a friend.

But she rarely comes right out and tells you exactly how she feels about you at a particular moment. Often she presents you with a Splenda smile and acts like she really cares about you, even claims she has your back.

Offstage, she sharpens her claws and is busy planning a mini cyber attack on you. She is super sneaky online. She cyber bullies you by posting something demeaning about you or by repeating something she's heard about you that's not good. And she can use ugly language and do whatever she feels like.

 NEW TEXT FROM LEANNA, 14: What we need, starting in like 5th or 6th grade, is a class that teaches us what's OK and what's way offensive 2 send.

Therefore, the term "frenemy" describes a girl who is sometimes for you and with you, and sometimes against you and who acts adversarial. You can really never tell with her, which puts you in a difficult position. Can you trust her, you wonder. Is she judging you superficially only, for instance, by whether you have an iTouch or not?

In fact, does she only like the girls that have the same Facebook theme as she does? Honestly, is her MySpace more important to her than you being present in her actual space?

Yes, you think one day. *No, she couldn't be like that— that's too shallow*, you think the next day. So the Cyber Frenemy is borderline in regard to being a friend. What she likes to use in her on-again, off-again friendly behavior toward you is the buffer that online chatter provides. She never comes right out and tells you that you don't matter to her; she shows her hidden animosity through her clicks. That's the very worst part about her, that she can be loving one day then cyber diss you the next day.

Facebook, MySpace, Twitter, and other accounts are all forms of Internet communication. They are social networking sites that can be super fun to describe your likes and dislikes and update your girlfriends and family. Too bad the Cyber Frenemy also has access to them.

 NEW TEXT FROM ORIANA, 14: My friends and I have been prank phone called and prank texted. It's a constant thing that can hurt your self-esteem and make you waste your time worrying.

And even if you don't have one of those accounts, she can still affect and annoy you. How? She can post something negative about you on her page. Or she can identify her good buds and leave you out. Or she can hint at a certain "annoying pest" she's sick and tired of and describe her in such a way that everybody thinks it's you, even if it isn't. That can ruin your day.

But if you allow even just one Cyber Frenemy control over your outlook and actions, then she is really in charge of your daily life and you're dancing to her tune.

Yes, Cyber Frenemies can be a negative influence on you because their comments, innuendos, and sly remarks can take up so much of your valuable time.

UNIVERSAL HIGH SCHOOL

Hadley is proud of the fact that she's never been caught texting at school, even though she does so every day. The rule is to have all cell phones and other electronic gadgets turned off once a student enters the building, unless it's an emergency. Hadley has a big emergency each and every day. Her mom forgot to increase the amount on her debit card, and her hair extensions cost a bundle. And her nail appointment is too close to her massage time. Her bangs are acting crazy and she needs a new flat iron ASAP.

Oh, there's so much on her mind. Even after homeroom, she is still texting her thumbs off. As she heads for first period, she almost bowls over three underclass girls. "Sorry," she says with a big smile, but doesn't even slow down.

Suze, one of the girls she almost knocked down, grew up next door to Hadley. They were real close at one time, but that was six months ago or six weeks ago—eons, anyway. High school is a battlefield.

As Hadley hustles into the classroom where the teacher has her back to the students while writing on the board, Hadley checks her latest voice mails. Nobody important, she thinks. Delete, delete. And what about this text from a new friend? Should she answer? No way, this girl made a better grade on the last AP history paper. Erase! All this is done with the sweetest smile in place.

That afternoon Hadley ditches practice and zooms home. *Yay, Mom and Dad are already here,* she thinks when she sees both their cars. But as Hadley enters by the back door, she hears yelling coming from the master bedroom. Her parents are having a big fight—again. Silently, she ducks into her room, her iPod blasting to drown out the screaming and what sounds like stuff being thrown.

Hadley wonders frantically where to go to get away from this WWIII. Maybe to Suze's house? As she slithers the patio door open, her mom appears, looking upset.

"Oh, hi Mom," Hadley says, feeling trapped. Darn, if she'd only been a few seconds faster.

"Hi Hadley," Mom says. "I had no idea you'd be home early."

"Practice was cancelled. Everything okay?"

"Everything's fine. Just fine."

"Really?" Hadley asks, her eyes watering up because besides being angry, Mom looks so sad.

Her mother notices the threatening tears. "Are you okay?"

"Sure," Hadley says, wipes her eyes, and glues on a huge smile.

The most important thing to remember is that underneath the Cyber Frenemy is a girl that is conflicted. She may want to be a friend, but experience has shown her that she can't let her guard down and be herself. She doesn't dare share with another girl if something isn't right. She really has nobody to unburden herself to because she's been taught that it's best to always present a happy face to the world, even if she has to fake it.

That leads her to smile at you while she is about to fib, fabricate, and file a super-critical post about you on her blog.

If she were a real friend, she would come up and inform you to your face what she finds so annoying about you or help you with good advice and show her support. She could even stop interacting with you altogether. But no, she pretends to be your friend and then cyber disses you all over the Internet.

Don't ever let that type of behavior make you suffer. Let's see if you can face down the Cyber Frenemy.

No matter what her history or home situation, the Cyber Frenemy comes across as a selfish and thoughtless girl who has one goal—to advance her objectives, to get to the top of her crew, even if that means ditching you. And since she's cyber smart, her hoped-for rising claim to fame is achieved by the use of the latest technology. And sadly, she's not alone. There are so many of her out there. The most prevalent type of Cyber Frenemy is the Cyber Excluder.

FAST QUIZ

Cyber Frenemy Susceptibility—How Vulnerable Are You?

1. The Cyber Frenemy e-mails everyone on the tennis team except you to stop by her house after practice for a snack and a chat. There is so much to discuss this season, what with the new uniforms, the new coach, and the tough schedule and all. To deal with this obvious exclusion, you:

   A. Buy the closest 7-Eleven out of all the snacks they have, take them to your room, and stuff your face with everything.

   B. Ask the Frenemy if you can please, please, please drop off some homemade goodies at her house. You're known for making the best lo-cal fudge bars. You also beg to be allowed to come over later and help clean up.

   C. Barge right into the gathering, hog all the food and drinks, and complain loudly about the stale crackers, the funny-tasting cheese, the flat soda— and the lame crew assembled there.

   D. Go home and have lots of fun doing your nails and picking out what to wear tomorrow. At the right time, you tell the coach that a new rule needs to be added to the handbook: Team parties should be for the whole team.

2. One of your friends calls and tells you that next week on Earth Day you're supposed to wear a green top to school, but to keep it a secret. Only those in the know are to supposed to know, nobody else. You:

   A. Do not utter a word about the message you got. Loose lips sink friendships.

   B. Run home to check your wardrobe. You don't have any green shirts or sweaters and you feel like maybe some of the other girls are in the same situation, so you buy a bunch of white t-shirts and stay up all night tie-dyeing them green. Then you hand the splotchy shirts out at school on the morning of Earth Day and feel hurt when the other girls refuse to put them on. What's wrong with them?

   C. Make a tub of green Jell-O and sling a handful at every girl not wearing green on Earth Day. So what if the green stains their tops and manes?

   D. Want to do something for Earth Day, but feel bad about purposely excluding other girls, so you do something positive about it. You get permission to plant a new maple tree in front of the school. That old site really needs sprucing up and you're going to see to it.

3. The Cyber Frenemy texts your best friends asking them to dress up and sit in the front rows of the auditorium, those designated for family and friends, at the dress rehearsal of the big play she's starring in. You don't get a

dress-code text reminder or an evite. How do you feel
and deal? You:

A. Convince yourself that bad cell service is to blame
   and complain to your e-mail and cell provider.
B. E-mail the Cyber Frenemy, asking if you can be
   the usher and remain standing in the lobby to
   guide any latecomers to their seats.
C. Dress in your cut-offs and post "Reserved" signs
   on every seat in the two first rows. Then you barge
   in with a crew of your own and make rude noises
   throughout the performance.
D. Skip the rehearsal, go to the premiere, and sit
   where your ticket indicates. If it's general admis-
   sion, you pick and choose. The middle section is
   usually the best one as far as acoustics are concerned. You thoroughly enjoy the play and are
   happy you came. You want your drama on stage,
   not among the audience.

4. You're nonstop IMing with your classmates while all of
   you are doing American history homework, like you do
   lots of times, when suddenly everyone logs off. Later
   you find out that the Cyber Frenemy lost her fave lip
   gloss, and all the other girls stopped IMing about the
   assignment to answer her frantic, demanding text SOS,
   which you never got. You:

   A. Stop working on homework immediately. You
      don't want to be the only one with her work com-

pleted when all the other girls won't have theirs done.

B. Drop everything and make a timeline throughout the day, plotting each hour the Frenemy still had her lip gloss and tracking down the exact moment when it got lost. You will not rest until you have zeroed in on the three most likely spots where the mishap might have occurred.

C. E-mail everyone incorrect homework answers ASAP. It's their loss, ditching you to look for some lame lip gloss. When the other girls blame you for their failing homework grades, you just smile and play dumb.

D. Finish your assignment alone, to the best of your ability. Sometimes working by yourself forces you to buckle down more, and you do now. When the other girls want to copy your answers, you refer them to the appropriate chapters, maybe even the relevant pages and paragraphs—but that's all.

Now let's find out how you did. Total up your answers.

ANSWERS

If you answered mostly As: Stop trying to seek cover in your room or in a crowd. Be proud of who you are, a smart girl with her own thoughts and opinions and so much to offer. Start by standing in front of the mirror and saying, "I have an opinion. This is what I think." Then pretend the mirror is an open window and looking through it, repeat your declaration. At the right moment, use these statements in public.

If you answered mostly Bs: It's time you had some surgery—the kind where you separate yourself from your unfriendly idol permanently. You know that she doesn't look out for you, so don't always follow in her wake. Make your own decisions; if they don't jive with hers, so what. She isn't the mold you have to imitate. Cookie-cutter behavior is for baking, not for basking in your own light.

If you answered mostly Cs: The world likes you, girl, but you don't always have to come out punching. You have so much leadership in you, but instead of really showing it, you use it for flashy showmanship. Of course, you can tread on other girls, but even though some of them may deserve it, there's no need to grind them in the dust. If you do, you will be covered with it.

If you answered mostly Ds: You have a good habit of looking at the big picture. You know that with a little forethought you can figure things out. Of course, it's nice to be respected by all the girls, even those with faux and foe feelings toward you, but you know that some of them are lagging in the maturity that kind of conduct requires. Growing up great is never a black and white process. So you give them a little more time to step up and stop cyber bullying others. Meanwhile, you're on to other productive pursuits that suit you!

If you have a mixture of As, Bs, Cs, and Ds: Review all of the above. There is obviously a little bit of everything in you, which is great. Now, can you work on dissing the Answer-A attitude and becoming more of a fan of the Answer-D attitude?

 NEW TEXT FROM ELORA, 17: I've been harassed over instant messaging since back in middle school. Girls can be very immature until they're about done with high school.

CYBER FRENEMY SMARTS: WHAT SHOULD YOU KNOW ABOUT THE CYBER FRENEMY?

Any group of girls has its share of cyber frenemies. But what's good about them is that you can easily spot them—all it takes is getting burned by them one time. What can you do to avoid even that one bad experience?

★ The Cyber Frenemy can come in many forms. She can be a girl just trying to show off, being accidentally unkind. As she grows up more and with your good influence, she'll start thinking before clicking mindlessly.

★ The Cyber Frenemy can also be the type of girl who's been waiting for the opportunity to up her self-esteem by lowering yours and that of others by acting unkind—purposely. The techno world to her is not an arena for unlimited learning and a great chance to expand her horizon; to her it is an arena of unlimited leaving-you-out communication and a great chance to make sure you know you've been left out. And everybody else knows, too.

★ There are various groups of Cyber Frenemies, for example the Side Chick and Social Climber. That is a girl clinging to the most popular chick in the school and desperately trying to hang on to her hard-won position. That means the Side Chick often has to do the dirty work for the top chick. Closely related are the Cyber Jibber-Jabber, the gossipy girl who loves getting the nasty word out about everyone, with the click of a mouse, of course.

★ What's worse: This type of gossipy Cyber Frenemy is a fan of CCing everyone. If you e-mail her something in haste, watch out. She spreads it across the World Wide Web faster than you can blink your eyes, and without your permission. This type of Cyber Frenemy has a little sister, the Cyber Drama Princess—a girl who bores everyone to death with the mega crises she creates over nothing and with the emotional cyber outbursts she loves. She's so into using exclamation points (!!!!!!!!), underlining, and using ALL CAPS. And oh, how she likes to text, text, text. She's the one for whom the term overtexting was invented.

The Cyber Frenemy is a girl who actually could be a good pal, but that's only an intermittent phase. Sure, like you, she is in the process of growing up, but she seems to have a harder time than you and your real friends. For the time being, she's in the grips of relational aggression, which fuels her mean messages, posts, or picture forwarding. Someday away from school, she could be among your best friends. Right now, however, she has no clue how to make real friends. Until she learns that, you need a quick solution to her and her mean cyber sisters.

RAPID RESPONSE: WHAT YOU SHOULD DO ABOUT THE CYBER FRENEMY?

Be careful around her—remember that you can't trust her and should weigh what you say. But once you know that, just be mindful about what you message her, what you e-send her, and what you tell her on the phone.

1. Treat the Cyber Frenemy more like a stranger, someone to be wary of. Know that everything posted online, whether it's on Facebook or via your e-mail account, can be considered a wide-open gathering of friends, but also of enemies. So never put anything out there that can be held against you or any picture that could be construed as something negative.

2. Keep a file of the Frenemy's offenses. This is for your protection. If they are minor, pay them no mind. So what if she cyber excludes you from a little get-together? You can't go to everything anyway, and you don't want to go to an event that's hosted by a girl that gets a kick out of being a digital mean chickadee.

Yet if the Frenemy goes too far, and her bugging you becomes a major annoyance, stop shrugging it off. Gather your best friends around you and hold an intervention with the Frenemy. Each one of you recites an instance where the Frenemy did something mean to you, then tell her how she's losing lots of good friends, unless she makes amends. Do this as kindly as possible.

3. Finally, learn to choose your friends more wisely. A Frenemy is no friend, unless she shapes up and acts right. You have it in your power to think about the Frenemy, help her to be a real friend, or end the relationship with her. There are thousands of girls out there who can be true to you; don't settle for a pain in the digital domain.

WHAT I WENT THROUGH—A REAL-LIFE STORY FROM KARI, 15

I love, well like, school and my life and all. Most times anyway. I have a bunch of real nice friends, they're my BFFs; we've been around each other since third grade, and we usually have lots of fun.

Not any more. Lately, I've gotten so unsure. It's mainly about this one girl, Kim. She has always been competitive with me, like she tries to beat me in everything which I used to think is good. It makes me try harder, and it's all in fun, like in basketball when she makes more free throws or in gym when I can do more push-ups.

Anyway, it's been going back and forth between us all these years, but now I don't know. When she does something better, we all clap. But when I do something better, she makes some snide remark about "letting me win," because it's good for me, because I'm Scarry Kari.

When I was five, my parents and I were in an accident and I still have a scar from it. It doesn't show in the winter, but in the summer when I get a tan, there's a thin white line on my left arm. You wouldn't notice it, but ever since Kim has started calling me Scarry Kari, I'm self-conscious about it. Even more upsetting is Kim acts like she really likes me to my face, but she uses the initials SK in her all e-mails and texts. And now all my other friends do the same thing when they message, and girls from other schools have picked it up. They call me Scarry Kari, Scary Scarry Kari, Way Scary Scarry Kari, stuff like that, when they post on Facebook.

And what do my friends do? They just laugh and laugh and laugh about it.

Dr. Erika's Response

What an awful way to act toward a friend. Labeling and nicknaming a girl for any reason—whether it's a physical thing or an orientation or a skin pigment or a name or ethnicity—is completely uncool. Only fools would do it and only foolish girls would imitate this bad behavior and laugh about it.

What the girls should have done is stand up for Kari and told Kim to stop the name calling. First, of course, Kari should've told Kim loud and clear, three times: My name is Kari, call me Kari, that's it. Nothing but Kari, okay? (BTW: You might think this is stooping to their level—but hey, sometimes, in a very rare case, you might really have to make a point!)

Fortunately, it's not too late for improving the failing grade, girls. All it will take is a few e-mails or posts to Kim addressing her as Crazy Kim or CK and she'll get the picture. Trust me, this approach works like a charm.

DEAR DIARY

Now that you have learned to identify the Cyber Frenemy and how vulnerable you are in regard to her, you know what course to take. And that is to put her in her place and reduce her effect on you. But what about what she did to you in the past?

It's time to get over those hurt feelings. So pull out your journal or pull up your personal blog and let the keys run wild and give your thumbs free reign. Let it all out, whatever you remember about the last time you were cyber teased. Include in the telling of every mean event what you felt, what you thought about it, how it might have hurt you, and how you dealt with the situation.

You did nothing? Okay then, now is the time to write what you wish you could've done, at the time or maybe later. How could you have better responded to the slight or slur, the teasing, or tormenting the Cyber Frenemy did to you?

Use your journal or blog to get rid of any hurt feelings you have about them, then forget about them and forge ahead. But before you log off, write three goals you have now and how not even an army of Frenemies can hold you back.

How fortunate you are living in the cyber age. You have—right at your fingertips—the ability to use the latest technology to do enormous good, for yourself and for others. You can get your school work done faster and better than any group of girls in the past. You can sign up for and support all sorts of good causes with a caring click. You can connect with family and friends in the most cutting-edge way. You are able to brighten a sick classmate's day or check up on an acquaintance you've lost touch with.

But what if you had a bad day and just want to do a little sniping and griping. In response to your nasty attitude, you decide to dabble in a little cyber meanness.

Rx: Chopping Chatter-tude

A chatter-tude can also be called a tit-for-tat-itude. In other words, this mood makes you want to get back at some girl. These are the times you neglect to think before you act, and say—or write—something you don't mean. How do you avoid that 'tude?

To stop it, at least one time a day:

1. Post something positive about a girl. Sure, it's a powerful feeling to tap out some "secret" you overheard or to text a stinging zinger to a girl you're jealous of, but this way your energy is better spent and you're not hurting anyone's feelings.

2. Ask yourself if you are so insecure that you need to control other girls by digital dissing them. Of course you're not. Whenever you feel the urge to be a

Frenemy online or on text, just pretend you are the girl being cyber gossiped about. And then cut it out—and concentrate on yourself.

3. Turn the Cyber Frenemy into a cyber friend by helping her get in touch with her genuine friendship side and ability and by changing the cyber topics and posts to encouraging ones. Help her—and yourself— avoid texting and tweeting anything that's not acceptable. Help her develop a more forgiving and less critical outlook, and yourself as well. Don't become a nit-picking cyber chick. On your chatter-tude days, give your texting digits a time-out. Rest your laptop and stop living on the Net. Great girls like you need some quiet time now and then to grow into the finest human beings they can become.

THE BOTTOM LINE

Often the Cyber Frenemy may not actually want to hurt you; she would never tell you off to your face! In fact, she may only want to enjoy the powerful feeling of deciding who's in or out of her cliques online. And most often, her desire to control you stems from a feeling of no control at home or from a feeling that you have something she doesn't or are something she is not. And how she wishes she were you!

So don't let any Cyber Frenemy detract from you and your time to shine, which is NOW. Identify what subtype she belongs to—most likely she has overlapping qualities.

She may be mainly into cyber excluding, cyber rumoring, cyber social climbing, or cyber name calling.

 NEW TEXT FROM KATE, 14: This girl I know is really into mean tweeting. She loves to label guys as "manorexic" and girls as "skinny britches" w/o the r. But she thinks she is so gr8.

No matter how the Cyber Frenemy shows her conflicted friendship feelings, the problem rests squarely on her shoulders. So choose your course of action, independent of her mean chatter-tude.

Always remember, happiness is not happenstance—it doesn't just pop up someday somewhere by chance. You have to make it happen, and that starts with being prepared to handle the Cyber Frenemy. You need to understand her, put up with her if you feel like it, pan her if you don't, and maybe even push her out of your life.

But you definitely can't allow her to be the center of your life. Just place her where she belongs, on the outer fringes of your wonderful circle of real friends and on the perimeter of your life. Yes, you may certainly consider being open to being her good friend, but only after she's gotten her act together. That means she melds her sweet fakey front with her true cyber persona, or vise versa. She needs to treat you like you deserve to be treated—with total respect, not with a faux smile and a cyber saber aimed at your back.

Chapter 8
The Cyber Pit Bully

WHAT MAKES A GIRL A CYBER PIT BULLY?

She looks just like any other girl in your school, but can be quiet in a group. Up close, some girls might consider her standoffish, but she makes up for that with her modest demeanor. She's really the opposite of a snobby chick; she's never obnoxious and dresses like she doesn't care that much. And she never participates in any mean chick conduct. In some ways, she seems more grown-up than other girls, and sports a bland facial expression, as if high school's only a way station for her. She's so eager to move on that she takes a load of advanced classes, but keeps it to herself. In fact, she's somewhat invisible. That's why it would be such a tremendous shock if the truth were known.

The truth is, she's a Cyber Pit Bully.

DEAR DR. ERIKA:

Last month at a flea-market sale, I found this cool Oscar de la Renta vintage dress that's all rhinestoney and looks so great on me. I told my friends about it and about me planning to wear it to the formal winter dance. That's a bigger deal at my school than the prom. Ever since, this awful picture has been floating around the Internet. It pops up everywhere. It shows me diving headfirst into an old dumpster.

I know where the picture is from. It got cell-phone cameraed during our fall cleanup at school. My best friend lost her keys and I was trying to dig them out of the trash for her. This photo might be a teeny bit funny if it didn't have this caption: "Caroline Shopping for the Big Dance."

~Caroline, 16

DEAR DR. ERIKA:

Help! I think I have a Facebook stalker. This girl I don't even know—I really have no idea who she is—goes through my FB pictures and writes nasty messages. And when I delete them, she does it even worse. I spend more time worrying about what mean stuff she puts out there about me next and checking up on that than I spend time doing my school work. Last week, I like acted like I was sick and stayed home. The next day there were messages about me being a loser that nobody liked. I really feel like I can't go on like this.

~Kristin, 14

FYI

The latest ways in which mean girls are mistreating other girls are via social media. While some of these mean cyber methods are mainly annoying and less worrisome, as mentioned in Chapter 7, many can be downright frightening. But with a little knowledge, you can not only protect yourself from the negative digital dirty deeds of others, but also make smarter decisions about choosing friends on the Internet and foster positive change.

So let's take a close look at the worst kind of girl cyber bullies and the horrible damage they do online or through texting. Can you believe it? Sometimes even the mean chicks' parents get into the hurtful cyber acts.

The most notable case of this was in the news: Thirteen-year-old Megan took a very tragic step after receiving a series of online insults. Later, the mother of Megan's former friend was charged with misdemeanor computer fraud in the case. She helped create a fake MySpace page for a teenage boy who befriended and courted Megan online—and then cruelly rejected her.

But even if an errant parent doesn't worsen the girl cyber meanness, a vicious click chick can do incredible harm all by herself. That's why she's called the Cyber Pit Bully.

In short, the Cyber Pit Bully is the worst cyber bully you'll ever run across, and the damage she can inflict—should she really target you—can disrupt your entire life.

Yes, one of the biggest menaces girls face today is escalating cyber bullying. With cyber bullying, real mean chicks have many new ways to exclude, diss, harass, and torment other girls through the Internet and cell phones.

 You have one new e-mail: I have been bullied through texts and MySpace. It's still going on. And the more I ignore it, the worse it gets. These girls are always after me. Do you know how horrible that feels? ~Shanise, 16

Whether the Cyber Pit Bully works alone or with others, if unchecked and not dealt with, any online harassment can lead the victims to cut school or become depressed.

Even if no serious outward consequences ensue, a tenacious Cyber Pit Bully can crush a girl's spirit for the moment, a week, a month, or more. Maybe even forever. The scars could be life changing, but once you look more closely at the Cyber Pit Bully, you'll find that she has scars, too, and maybe that's why she acts the way she does.

You don't think the Cyber Pit Bully is hurting? Let's check in on Jada.

UNIVERSAL HIGH SCHOOL

Jada felt butterflies in her stomach as she crept into her first-period class, economics. She had plenty of reason for the attack of nerves that made her queasy. She wanted so bad to hide under her desk in back and shrink herself so teeny-tiny that Ms. Olsen wouldn't notice her. It was always the worst luck to be called on first when major projects were due, and today was one of those horrible, dreadful days. The class has been assigned to pretend they were starting their own business and to prepare a business plan: Create a brand-new product or brand, describe it in detail, make a prototype of it, plus write up a cost analysis, report on future earnings, and stuff like that. Then each student had to get up and pitch their idea to the whole class.

Yikes, that was the very worst thing. Jada hated the idea of having all her classmates stare her down, roll their eyes, even burst out roaring at her lame idea, which she had majorly slaved over.

She is a shy girl, but liked by a lot of kids. Always quiet, but ready to help you in a pinch, she was the kind of girl that was sure to get voted friendliest in her senior year.

The classroom door cracked and Ms. Olsen strolled in, followed by the Superintendent. Jada heaved out her pent-up breath. This was great news: a guest speaker, so no presentations today! Then she heard her name called. Her face feeling hotter than a roaring wild fire, she stumbled to the front of the room. But after clearing her throat, she plunged right into giving her report and extolled the plus points of her new teen fashion line—HGHB. She showed off a jean skirt she had hand sewn and wore. She explained her market research, the production cost, future income projections, and so on—all without looking at a single piece of paper.

The class gave her a huge round of applause. She returned to her seat, face still burning red, but this time from pride. Turned out the school superintendent had come to serve as a judge—like on *American Idol.* "That was perfect," she said, smiling. "I'm impressed. So what does your label mean?"

Jada smiled, too. "Well, BCBG (Bon Chic Bon Genre) is doing so well. Their name means 'Good Style Good Class,' so I named my line HGHB for 'Happy Girl Happy Brand.'"

"What a wonderful idea," the Superintendent said, clapping. "I like it, I really like it." The rest of the day, Jada sailed through school like a kite on a breeze. Only when she got home did her demeanor change. Luckily, nobody was home, but she still flinched. Everyone in her family had such a rotten temper. Once she put up a poster of Brad Pitt and Dad slapped her. Another time her brother found a guy's picture in her purse and kicked her shins, calling her a slut. And her mother had a habit of pinching her, for no reason.

So Jada lived on pins and needles all the time, never knowing from where and when the next blow will come. She microwaved herself a pasta dish and scurried to her room, making sure the drapes were drawn and the door double locked. Then she read over the glowing written evaluation Ms. Olsen had given her. Oh, how she savored all the compliments her classmates had showered her with. They told her how her HGHB report really rocked, how creative she was, how super prepared. Some girls even asked where they could buy a skirt like the one she wore.

Happy Girl Happy Brand? Yeah, right. Jada booted up her computer and logged on to Facebook. She was going to mess with a few people she'd noticed weren't clapping very loudly for her. Then she was going to e-mail a wimpy chick in her class from her fake account, pretending to be the guy she likes! Nobody knows what HGHB really stands for: "Hurt Girl Hurts Back."

If you can, keep in mind that underneath the Cyber Pit Bully is a girl who may have started out not so different from you, but then something bad happened. Somehow, something in her mind got twisted, and now she's showing the effects of that. Don't worry about running into lots of Cyber Pit Bullies, but you can count on the fact that in every big school there's at least one. She may even lurk in smaller schools. So how can you protect yourself? Take this quiz to see what you can do to keep from becoming a victim of the Cyber Pit Bully.

FAST QUIZ

Cyber Pit Bully Susceptibility—How Vulnerable Are You?

1. You get a threatening e-mail from a girl telling you to "leave her man alone," or else. At first, you don't even know what the girl is talking about. Then you remember that yesterday you said hi to a new guy in your homeroom. You:

   A. Wear your most unflattering outfits and change your seat in every class so you're as far away as possible from any guys. You don't even glance at them, neither in the halls nor in the cafeteria or on the bus. Guys are nothing but trouble.

B. E-mail the girl back, apologizing profusely for speaking to "her man," and asking if you can treat them to pizza after school—just for the two of them alone, so they can cement their relationship.

C. Write back at once, "Or else what, huh? Huh?" Last time you checked, nobody owned anybody, and you'll prove it. This cute little guy is your next target.

D. Reply, "I was always taught that it's polite to greet someone back who greets you first."

2. You get a text from an unknown source, calling you every curse word in the world. You:

A. Stare at your phone like it's a viper, power it off as fast as you can, and hide it under your bed so you don't have to see it.

B. Flush, blush, and hang your head in shame. Then you slowly analyze each derogatory word, trying to figure out what you could've done wrong to deserve being called a skanky *!@+&. Maybe if you changed your behavior? You're so sorry you offended somebody. Now how can you act better from now on?

C. Rack your brain for the rudest, crudest curses you've ever heard. Then text them to the sender every ten minutes around the clock.

D. Assume the message wasn't meant for you. Still, you don't want even the slightest association with this toilet texter, so you block the number.

3. Your group wants to start a new tradition, called Sexting Sunday. Once a month, each girl is supposed to take a revealing photo of herself and send it to a random guy at school. Then watch for the hilarious fallout the following Monday. You:

A. Don't want any part of this. So when the day comes, you stay in your room all day, curled up in a fetal position with a cozy blanket wrapped around you.

B. Immediately beg your mom to take you shopping at Victoria's Secret—no more ratty undies for you. You don't know if you will even bare a lacy bra strap or advertise the top of your thong in your risqué photo shoot, but being prepared is never wrong.

C. "Accidentally on purpose" text this idea to the captains of the various sports teams, and invite the guys to get the ball rolling. You call it "Boxer Shorts or Whitey-Tighties?" In other words, "Show me yours, I'll show you mine" is your motto.

D. Think this is a bad idea and speak up. If the other girls still don't seem to have a clue about what could turn into sexual harassment, if taken too far, or even into child porn—depending on the age of the participants—you find another group to hang with ASAP. First, you notify the school administration about this anonymously. Just drop a note to

them and another note to the guidance department as a backup.

4. There is chat-room talk about a "fight club" being
started among the kids in your city. A representative of
each school is supposed to meet behind the football
field of your school on Saturday afternoon and slug it
out. You've been asked to videotape the event. You:

A. E-mail your ailing Aunt Alice, asking if you can
visit for the weekend. Please!

B. Have your video equipment professionally
inspected and buy more memory. This costs
plenty, but what can you do? Your career as famous
videographer is about to be launched. You are so
excited.

C. Start working out with free weights and do some
major sparring so you can be ready. Hey, you've
always wanted to be on YouTube, and here's your
chance.

D. Immediately tip off the administration, the guidance department, the security officer, and your
parents. You're not going to stand by when a
potentially dangerous activity is being planned.
Somebody could get seriously injured, but not
with you knowing about it.

Now it's time to find out how you did. Total up your
answers.

ANSWERS

If you answered mostly As: Always fading into the woodwork might work for wallpaper, but it doesn't work for girls. You are filled with so much potential and terrific talent, so stop quivering and shivering when an issue comes up that requires you to take a stand. The more often you refuse to run away, the more good you'll get done.

If you answered mostly Bs: Sure, it's good to fall in line sometimes, but not every time. Be proud and claim your strong points. It's time for you to take a chance and advance out of the shadow of other girls.

If you answered mostly Cs: Is it because you feel you're not as good as other girls that you always come out spoiling for a fight and wanting to butt heads? Why is it every time you have to make a decision you charge first and then ponder what you did? Take a deep breath and consider all possibilities before immediately declaring an all-out war. You have a solid backbone, now all you have to do is slow down, use your mind muscles, and hone your tactics and score.

If you answered mostly Ds: You have the proper balance of get up and go, guts, and caring for others 'tude. You aren't intimidated by any cyber silliness or even the biggest digital Pit Bullies. Of course, some mean-girl demeanor, online or off, can hurt, but not for long because you think it through and take the right steps to shrink the cyber teasing, taunting, and tormenting. And you help other girls and try to improve the world.

If you answered a mixture of As, Bs, Cs, and Ds: Review all the answers. Obviously, there's a little bit of everything in you, which is great. Now can you work on having a little more of that D attitude?

CYBER PIT BULLY SMARTS: WHAT SHOULD YOU KNOW ABOUT THE CYBER PIT BULLY?

You can't stop all crazy ideas spawned on the Net and all the wild online behavior and their outcomes around you, but you can be informed about what may motivate the Pit Bully's sometimes sketchy behavior:

★ The Cyber Pit Bully's motivation may be to get back at people who hurt her, but maybe she can't get revenge on the people that did it. Or maybe she doesn't even realize where her pain stems from because she has repressed it—so far—so she's paying her hateful and vengeful feelings forward by expressing them toward other girls.

★ Know this: The Cyber Pit Bully is hurting. Somewhere in her life, sad things have happened to her or are happening still. No girl whose life has been good or pretty good will purposely try to cyber destroy another girl with a Pit Bully frame of mind.

★ Delving into this mean cyber girl's history and helping her heal is the job of people who get paid for this sort of work. Know there are a host of professional helpers in all school systems, so there is lots of hope. Tell them about the Cyber Pit Bully. Meanwhile, your most important task is looking after yourself.

But what about right now? What can you do, should the Cyber Pit Bully pick on you?

RAPID RESPONSE: WHAT YOU SHOULD DO ABOUT THE CYBER PIT BULLY

You have several options to deal with the Cyber Pit Bully and take away her ability to sink her touch-pad teeth into you. Try these and feel empowered:

1. Print out or save any threats or mean statements you get—all the nasty e-mails, posts, or demeaning photos. But don't be overly sensitive and misinterpret the words or pictures—only document what was truly malicious.

2. It's best not to jump to conclusions and to first pause and ponder what cyber meanness you think is going on. Learn to distinguish a not-so-nice remark from a serious threat. Get the opinions of your friends on the issue, but in the end, always let your instinct be your guide. If you feel like something is a threat, then it is.

3. Immediately inform your parents, guidance counselor, and school resource officer about any cyber threat. Also, check your school's handbook. Are there guidelines for acceptable online, text, and social media communication? If not, get busy coming up with some really good rules. Every school needs a blogging and networking policy that all girls can follow. Responsibility is the key word. That means you need to be responsible in your digital communications and you expect others to be as well.

Never count on anything in cyberspace remaining anonymous or staying a secret. The Internet is like a lit-up glass house. Everybody can peek in anytime.

WHAT I WENT THROUGH—A REAL-LIFE STORY FROM RACHEL, 17

This year cyber bullying has been in the news a lot.

And when this stuff was on the news, we all talked about it in school. It was on my mind constantly, all this cyber bullying, which caused all this trouble. I felt so sorry for these girls that had done nothing wrong and yet they were targeted on Facebook, MySpace, and with mean texting and tweeting. They were all the victims of mean cyber chicks and hurtful clicks.

And then it happened to me.

I'm a senior and have a gazillion things to do. Like for instance, I'm the editor of our yearbook, which comes out in book form and online. I've got all sorts of big plans for after high school, but it all came crashing down on me like a house of cards. I'd been pushing myself with all the AP papers that are due and several killer exams coming up. That meant getting hardly any sleep and no time to eat. Plus the biggest track meet of the year was that Friday—where Coach expected me to set a new school record in the hurdles, so I can go on to State.

Well, by that Thursday I'd had it. All this pressure, I felt like I was being squashed by a heard of elephants. One more little thing—anything!—and I was going to scream.

It was a big thing, instead, and it happened in my favorite class, Advanced Journalism. My job was to proofread the final layouts and ad copy for the yearbook. The publishing company had sent not only our proofs but also those for the other high schools in the area. That was a mistake, but cool. I could check out what their designs were like, what businesses supported them with ads—when it hit me like a speeding train. In my advertising layouts as well as those for the other schools, was a big picture of me in my bikini bottom, with my top off and my back to the camera. Without my name, but with this copy printed across my picture: Don't Be a Loser, Buy a Yearbook!

This was the most embarrassing thing that could've happened. I knew I would never ever get over it. I remembered exactly when this snapshot was taken—on our spring break—but it was only for fun. And I held a towel in front of me, so it was really nothing. But some incredibly mean chick that's not even from our school used her cell phone to take my picture, cropped it to look like a legitimate ad, and forwarded it to the yearbook company, asking them to print it. How could she do that to me?

Suddenly, I snapped. I jumped up and ran out of the room. The other kids were stunned. Ms. Givens yelled at me to stop, but I couldn't. My heart was feeling like a NASCAR race, my face burned, like on fire. I raced straight home.

I flew into my room, headed for my walk-in closet, and frantically dug through my accessory collection until I found it—my skinny new red Prada belt. I tested it, it was strong, and I was actually thinking of hurting myself with it.

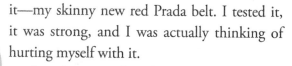

Just then, two friends from my journalism class burst through my front door and rushed up to my room. They knew how upset I was, and had come to check up on me. They freaked out when they saw me with the belt, but lied for me when we went back to school. They said I was about to faint, so I ran home so I wouldn't fall in school. They made me promise to tell my mom, which I did, so I could get some help, which I did. Then the girls tracked down the evil b-tch who had taken the picture, turned her in, and got her backside severely punished by her school. Then they redid the offensive ad.

Dr. Erika's Response

These girls were real friends. A real friend doesn't stand by when a friend is in pain—especially not when she may hurt herself. And this spirit of being there for another girl will get them far in the future. So we respect and honor them, and advise them to urge the girl who wants to hurt herself to see the guidance counselor ASAP.

DEAR DIARY

Now that you know about the rare but malicious Cyber Pit Bully and your susceptibility to her, you might feel bad because maybe you've had similar feelings about getting back at some girls who deserved it. If that's true, keep a log and record how many days in a row you feel like hating on another girl and why you feel this way. If you can, write about when you first had this spiteful feeling toward other girls. Did they really do something to you? And if they didn't, then who did? Who has been mean to you?

Just tap the computer keys and let it all out. But don't count the days that you have a fleeting mean thought; count only the days that the mean thought expressed itself in a mean text or rude message or inappropriate phone call or mean post. Write about all that anger that's built up in you.

Then pretend to have some good feelings about other girls—just act like you like them. For the moment, this may be wishful thinking, but practice typing something nice about other girls. Describe something sweet you might or could do for them. Who knows, maybe with time the good feelings toward them will become reality.

And as soon as possible, get rid of any mean posts, bad pictures posted, mean-spirited online words, or rumors—in other words, instead of house cleaning, do some hate cleaning. You don't ever want anything floating around in cyberspace that bears your negative imprint. You want your words to be warm and friendly, not harmful and frosty. So in your diary, write about your plan to de-mean cyberspace as much as you can. Besides progressing yourself, you want to help other girls progress, too, not hurt them. And then share any of your log entries that worry you with a trusted friend, your favorite teacher or coach, your guidance counselor, your mom, dad, sister, brother, aunt, uncle, or grandparents—in other words, your support network.

Don't have a support network? Build one now, by spelling out in your diary what kind of helpful network you'd like to have. Describe the traits you'd love in a close girlfriend. Then use the Net to connect with girls on the grow like yourself around the world. Nix the mean net chicks; start a kindness forum and blog about all of the positive stuff you do and that has been done around you. Exchange cyber hints of helpfulness. Online, meet and greet girls who are pushing themselves to explore positive avenues. Band and bond with other strong girls in cyberspace—you are one of them. It's always a good time for e-complimenting or sending a fun e-card!

FAB FIXES FOR WHATEVER ATTITUDE AILS YOU

What's so wonderful about growing up is that each second, minute, hour, or day brings with it an opportunity for positive growing and real glowing. And for dissing and dismissing any negatives standing in your way. You know the great feeling you have when you really focus on moving forward and hurtling over something not so hot, maybe a concept in class that you didn't understand at first or a brand-new subject that seemed daunting to start with.

It's the same thing with certain aspects of your personality. Some of them may need a little tweaking or adjusting, like parts of your attitude. On some days, some segment of it may go astray; you may feel real anti other girls.

So step up to bat and hit this type of attitude out of the ball park, especially if it seems to be a Cyber Pit Bully-tude.

Rx: Banishing Cyber Pit Bully-tude

A Cyber Pit Bully-tude is when you want to cyber bully another girl as horribly as you can, and you want her pain to be your gain. This can occur when you feel you need to control another girl in the worst way. There may be deep-seated reasons for feeling this way, and they need to be addressed. There are many professionals who'd love to help you; just dash off a note to your guidance counselor asking for an appointment.

Meanwhile, what can you do on your own to banish any signs of Cyber Pit Bully-tude? Check out these top tips and make them work for you. Every day:

1. Take out your angry feelings in exercise. Hit the treadmill running, push that weight machine, do crunches until you can't do any more. Make sure you sweat out your mad feelings.

2. Think about taking a course in anger management. Read up on some of them first. Maybe your school or a school in your area offers one. And don't worry, some anger can actually be good. It can propel you on to great art or super academic achievement or extraordinary athletic success. That means you're taking the anger in you and making it work for you.

You're using it as a springboard to vault high into the sky of greatness. But anger directed at others is useless, nonsensical, and detrimental to your friendships, health, happiness, and fabulous future. Don't let your anger become a danger to you!

3. Just like any bad habit, don't let the unhealthy habit of extreme cyber bullying settle in and control you for days, months, years, even decades. Otherwise, an outlook of hate can become your fate, and that is never a good thing. You see, if hate drives you, you're never truly in control. You're like a mindless machine being driven by detrimental urges, and that takes away from the real you, the great you, the best you! It also detracts from your interactions with others, and from your successful future and life.

You want to be blessed with the best, not burdened by the worst. So if you feel a serious Cyber Pit Bully-tude claiming you—if you feel serious *schadenfreude* ("glee when another girl feels pain or gets hurt or fails or falls or flunks or is in a fiasco"), then get busy and banish that mean attitude. Make it a point to support other girls in small ways and in big ones.

THE BOTTOM LINE

In regard to any Cyber Pit Bullies, there are other important things you should do: Never share too much about yourself online, so it can't come back to haunt you. Don't post any personal info on the web, and always use complex passwords and change them frequently. Also, Google yourself once a month to see if something negative has been posted about you, then remove it or have it removed.

 NEW TEXT FROM BETH, 16: I know 1 girl that ignored the way embarrassing pictures of her online and she didn't get into her fave college 'cause of it.

Don't let any Cyber Pit Bully ruin your future. The best way to prevent this is to adopt a simple three-step procedure like the one you learned when you were little. So you won't get burned by the Cyber Pit Bullies: stop, block, and report.

* ★ Stop and think about whatever cyber or digital meanness you come across before doing anything.
* ★ Block the source immediately.
* ★ Report the cyber bullying to a parent, teacher, or other trusted adult.

Other safe cyberspace hints: Never e-mail when you're furious; count to fifty or 100, and cool off first. Don't participate in mean Internet polling, such as when you're asked who the biggest floozy or flunky is in your school. Don't open e-mails sent by a known mean chick. Don't click on any porn or other junk e-mail or attachments or on pictures sent from an unknown source.

Also, watch out for girls impersonating others, even you. Be aware that someone might pose as your friends or as your mom or dad. And don't get caught up in proxy bullying—passing on cyber hate mail. No forwarding mean messages or rumors either, and watch out for mass text attacks—those in which girls might send hundreds of messages to you, running up your phone bill. Finally, investigate whether there's a preventive course you can take.

Remember, you may not have all the power *yet*, but you have some power, so wield it. One thing that's fun to do is "third" your money. That means take a third of your money and save it for the future. Take the second third and use it for the good of other girls. Ask your guidance counselor if you might chip in for another girl's SAT or ACT fees, if she needs financial assistance. Then take the last third of cash and go insane crazy with it, spending it on yourself any way you choose.

Do the same thing with your free time, especially on weekends: Use one-third for school work or reading ahead; another third for doing some good around the house, like chores or for a community cause; then use the last third exclusively for yourself.

Whether you're a Cyber Pit Bully victim or have Cyber Pit Bully tendencies, you've been hurt, so pamper yourself. Take a deluxe bath with apricot body wash, soothing songs, lilac bath salts, even a candle. Shop for a tiny item in your fave color—a bracelet, headband, silk flower, or a sash. Spoil yourself with a comfort-food snack. Read a fun book and dote on yourself with a dose of daring daydreaming.

You will feel so much better—more healed or less in need of cyber harming other girls. You want to live your best life and are determined to do so. So carry out some planned acts of kindness in cyberspace. For every cyber meanness you find directed at a girl, direct an act of cyber kindness to her. E-invite her to a club that's making good things happen; e-ask her advice; post nice things on her Facebook; make her MySpace a place for positive pictures and points; tweet about her triumphs.

Never doubt that a thoughtful, strong girl like you can change the cyber world—you are that girl. You can change yourself, you can change other girls, and you can change your life. Smile a genuine smile that comes from loving who you are and knowing you have big goals and being sure you can handle even the worst Cyber Pit Bullies. Know that coping with and conquering them makes you stronger.

Part II
Standing Up for Yourself

Chapter 9
The Power of One

WHAT IS THE POWER OF ONE?

Here's a clue—it starts with you! All it takes is one girl to change the climate in your school and start to do something about this mean chick behavior we've been hearing so much about.

Sure, we know that boys can be mean, too, but it seems that our schools are better equipped to deal with mean-guy actions and infractions. In fact, teachers pass on information about which boys tend to fight from grade to grade. Therefore, administrators and counselors keep a special eye on them and make sure the most aggressive boys get placed in classes where they are separated from each other.

Truth be told, whole school communities band together to remove any triggers or inconveniences from potentially violent boys. And numerous teachers tiptoe around them, while everyone heaves a sigh of relief when those boys, known to be bullies, act relatively peaceful. "We're so glad you're showing a little improvement, Bobby," is the attitude of the school office. But the same special allowances are rarely made for girls. With your help, all of that can change. All you have to do is discover the Power of One.

DEAR DR. ERIKA:

When I first started middle school, other girls picked on me because of my size, just because I was a little bigger than they were. At that age, I didn't know anything about wearing only the name-brand clothes and I didn't worry about being skinny; that was the last thing on my mind. I was just ready for recess so I could run outside and play with my friends. When the teasing started, I was crushed. I will always remember the harsh words and the emotional pain I felt from it.

Today I know how to stand up for myself very well. I do not let things get to me as easily as I used to, and I do not give the smaller worries a bigger shadow. I try to be myself, and doing that has gotten me further than anything.

And I'm proud to say that my waist size has no effect on my self-esteem at all! Most important, I try to surround myself with girls who are positive and who set goals for themselves and their future. I think that's the best way—keeping away from girls that say negative comments about others.

In the end, you learn to be an all-around nice person.

~Shea, 16

FYI

Just because girls don't often duke it out physically doesn't mean they don't have feelings: feelings of disappointment, of anger, and of rage. Also, just because girls in general seem to hold in their negative emotions better doesn't mean that schools should simply overlook them. But they often do, and that makes the discontent simmer and stew below the surface of the girl world. In other words, it's there but it hasn't been openly acknowledged.

 NEW TEXT FROM NINA, 17: I fight with girls over Facebook and texting a lot. What's wrong with that? It's not like I punch them in the head.

You know that's not okay, and now you know that you can do something about it. You picked up this book; that means you have decided to do something about it. Good for you.

So now, focus on yourself. Think about yourself and all you can do, all that's deep inside you. What a wealth of abilities you have! You can form opinions, change your mind, ponder this and that, and ponder it some more the next day.

Rapid Response: What You Can Do to Promote the Power of One

1. Be sure that you're doing well. Are you happy most days? Are you content with your grades most days? There's always going to be a class or two that makes you groan every time you think about it. What a great place to start with the Power of One! Set a goal. Give yourself a challenge and rise to achieve it. Maybe it's as small as making sure you get your homework done every night. Or maybe it's as large as acing that final. Remember, it's not a competition. The other girls can look out for themselves in this. These are your goals and yours alone. Just be sure to do your best, no matter what.

2. Then think about your life outside school. There's a whole world out there for you to explore. What are you doing when you're not in school? Are you having fun, getting exercise, hanging with your buds as much as possible? With so many things to do in school every day, it's easy to forget that one of the best parts of being a girl is kicking back and having a good time. Be sure to work some fun into your schedule. You'll thank yourself for it later.

3. Are you helping others both in and out of school? Maybe it's time to think about some volunteer activities that help your community. How about volunteering for a nature project? How about doing what you can to help with the green effort, you know the reusing of materials and not wasting precious

resources? Is your school doing something along those lines? If so, get involved! If not, talk to a teacher or guidance counselor about starting an organization dedicated to the cause. You can also help out at the local center for the arts. By lending a helping hand to your classmates and your community, you are helping spread positive power through the girl world and beyond.

Whatever you attack first, remember you really are a powerhouse of one. But before you can change anything for the better, sometimes you may have to straighten out something that's not so nice about yourself, like Ginnie did.

WHAT I WENT THROUGH—A REAL-LIFE STORY FROM GINNIE, 18

When I started junior high, I was very skinny. I had plenty of friends; I hung out with the popular girl clique and got along with everyone. Only one time did I get in trouble. That was when one of my friends started calling me "Stick."

One day I couldn't take it anymore; I had had enough. I just snapped. I threw this girl down, jumped on top of her, and started hitting her in the face. The teachers ran over, pulled me off of her, and proceeded to take me to the office. Somehow, I managed to get loose and jumped back on top of her again. I felt so much better after that. I couldn't wipe the smile off my face and had no regrets about the trouble I was in because this was the first time I had ever defended myself.

The next year, I gained weight when my parents got divorced. I was depressed 24/7. I wanted things back the way they used to be. Nobody knew what was going on because I didn't want anyone to know. I didn't know how to handle all the emotions I was feeling, so I lashed out at everyone. I turned into a real brat, acted like I was better than everybody, and stomped my foot when things didn't go my way. I slammed doors, and I also did the name calling, the teasing, and the rumor spreading. I acted like a real *$?&!. One teacher noticed it and sent me to the school counselor, and I told her about my issues.

From then on, every week she checked up on me. She would always tell me if I felt real bad or mad or depressed to come talk to her about it first before doing anything. She said I had to learn about what made me so down and angry and how to deal with it. Her invitation, and knowing that she was there for me if no one else was, saved me.

Dr. Erika's Response

See how Ginnie empowered herself? She didn't like the way she was acting—which was totally unacceptable—so she got some help. By talking to the school guidance counselor about her problems, she realized she wasn't alone and that she was stronger than she thought. She started dealing with her sadness over her parents' divorce and realized that taking it out on her classmates was not the way to go.

SMART STRATEGIES

Now it's time to look at some smart strategies to get you through the day. These strategies come from real girls all over the country—girls just like you. Check out what they have to say.

Smart Strategy #1

Caryn, 13, shares: "Once I was picked on by this girl about my weight. So I was thinking: Why don't I start a girls' workout club and hand out nutrition info at every school?"

Caryn has a good point. A healthy body and mind go hand in hand. It's medically proven that just thirty minutes of exercise a few times a week is not only good for your body, it's also good for your mood. It can improve your focus, your mood, and even your sleeping patterns. Perhaps if the girls at your school had a workout club, they would feel better about themselves, which means they won't feel the need to tease each other. Then, rather than competing about clothes, cliques, or gossip and jealousies on Facebook, girls can compete through sports, which is much healthier for your mind—and your body!

Why not try to form a workout club in your own school? Check with your PE teacher or someone else you trust and find out what you can do to get a club like this going in your own school. If working out isn't your thing, there are tons of clubs you could organize—maybe a roller-blading club, a literary magazine, or a homework network on the web, even a game club where girls could get together to play Wii tennis or something else fun.

Smart Strategy #2

Rene, 15, wrote: "I accidentally hurt a girl's feelings when I thought we were just joking around. I know it's not right to pick on anyone. So I thought to myself, why don't we have a short course, like a couple hours at the beginning of every school year, where they teach us the difference?"

Great idea, Rene. The difference between harmless teasing and hurling hateful words should be taught, and not just at your school but everywhere the world over. Talk to a teacher or maybe even your principal about having a course like this. Or, if you like, maybe you can start such a program yourself.

"Me," you say? Yes, you! You know you've got the Power of One.

Start by going to the librarian at your school and telling her what you have in mind. She can network with other school librarians and order books or pamphlets or DVDs on this topic for you. Also, check with your guidance counselor and ask for his or her help. Then, maybe at the beginning of the school year, you can visit various homerooms or classes and tell them about the course. Or maybe you can pass on information about the topic to teachers and they can use it as part of class discussion. Education is power, and by educating your peers about the ways of mean chicks, mean tricks, and hurtful clicks, who knows, you could be the start of a wonderful change.

If having a class is not your thing, maybe you can institute a Planned Acts of Kindness Day. Talk to your teachers about having a day that promotes girl-to-girl kindness and awareness of mean chick behavior. This can be a day dedicated to using cyberspace and text messages only in a kind, supportive way. Just one day to get the word out that all girls are okay, no matter how different they are.

Smart Strategy #3

Megan, 14, says, "It's wrong to pick on girls to hurt their feelings, so why don't our teachers make us stop it? Why aren't there any rules posted about it? And why don't we have announcements over the intercom every day, reminding us about the dangers of traditional and cyber bullying?

"Until there is a way for girls to speak out against obstacles such as gossiping, rumors, and name calling, there won't be a solution to the problem."

There are tons of fun ways to express yourself through art, so why not use it to help improve the girl world?

First, get permission to post signs and banners on the walls. Then, put your head together with some friends or classmates and create a message that's impossible to ignore. Create posters, banners, flyers, maybe even draw a cartoon for your school's newspaper about the dangers of bullying. Work up a "Warning: This Is a Bully-Free Zone" poster or "Mean Texting Is Demeaning," then make copies and tack them on the bulletin boards of every classroom.

Talk to the teacher you admire the most; get her input on a creative handout you could come up with on the types and warning signs of girls' aggressiveness and cyber bullying. Then pass it out, after getting the okay from the school administration first, of course.

By using some of these Smart Strategies or by creating your own, you are empowering yourself and passing that power on to other girls who need it. You're moving and improving your surroundings. Good for you!

FAB FIXES FOR WHATEVER ATTITUDE AILS YOU

Some days you wake up, hear the sounds of your family members moving through the house, maybe somewhat sleepily, and you jump up, beating them to everything—the bathroom, the kitchen, the newspaper on the driveway. Oh, this is a day you feel you can move mountains. That's how good you feel. Nothing can stop you, not even the thought of a long and tough schedule ahead.

So really, you know you can do it and do it well, or at least as well as you can, which is great. It means you have a case of can-do attitude—wow! That's the right attitude to have. It's easy to put into action because it's built on what you already have so much of—your aptitude.

So reinforce it. How? Just use this prescription tailored to you.

Rx: Amping Up Your Aptitude

Three times a day:

1. Repeat out loud (when you're alone): "I can and will make a difference!"
2. Lie on top of your bed, close your eyes, and envision yourself succeeding in life, really succeeding big

time. Imagine that you can accomplish anything you want. And especially imagine what you can do right now to help your school become free of mean chick behavior.

3. Start a girl-to-girl kindness chain. Choose the most "blah" day at your school, like Mondays. Then decide that on this day you say only nice things to other girls and about them. Encourage your friends to do the same, and to text, forward, and e-mail only words of positivity. Just have this one day a week be totally free of backstabbing, gossiping, teasing, and cutting down other girls, and all the prank phoning and mean posting on Facebook and Twitter. Think of how many other girls you can help.

THE BOTTOM LINE

So, what's the bottom line on the Power of One?

★ You have so much power inside you. Think about it and be grateful to be who you are. Then use it— this awesome power. It's such a great feeling to use your Power of One for yourself and for others.

★ Start with a small project that represents that Power of One you have; next time, tackle a bigger problem and just think of how many girls will benefit from what you're doing.

★ Then aim for something even bigger to do— something you can spend some time on, maybe something that will change an outdated school rule or add a new one, update a program or start a new one. Read over the section in your school handbook that deals with cyber aggression and see what's been left out. Use all your creativity and smarts, those in your head and in your heart!

Check out how Anna Liu overcame her problems and worked to make a difference:

"When I was thirteen I had to wear glasses because I am nearsighted. At first, I was really excited about having glasses. I went to the doctor's office to pick them up. I tried them on to make sure they fit, and they did! I began to get numerous compliments from the doctors and even people I had never met. My confidence rose to the extreme.

"When I returned to school that following Monday, before I could reach my classroom, I began to hear laughter and my classmates shouting, 'Is that her with those glasses?'

"I just knew they were referring to me, but I didn't let it get to me at first. But as the day went on, the laughing got worse. I lost it and started to cry. This one girl in particular looked at me and said, 'Stop crying, you already look like a freak!'

"In anger, I snatched the glasses off and broke them. I had taken all the embarrassment that I could take for one day. When I got home, my mother asked me where my glasses were.

"'Broke,' I said. 'Nobody liked them and people made fun of me. They laughed and called me names. I don't ever want to wear glasses again.'

"After my mother embraced me and explained to me that no matter what people thought about my new look I would always be beautiful, she called the eye doctor and made an appointment to get brand-new glasses.

"That next week, I had a new attitude about my glasses and I didn't care what people said or thought! And then I wrote about it for my school paper, and several other girls came up and said they saved this issue because it helped them when they were mean-teased. Now they knew they were not alone. I didn't know a little old essay of mine could do so much good. I mean, it was just me doing it."

Chapter 10
The Power of Several

WHAT IS THE POWER OF SEVERAL?

The power of several is the wonderful, amazing, and exponentially increased strength that comes from two or more girls banding together to do some good. "You know what would really be great?" one of the girls I interviewed for this book asked me.

She had my full attention: "No, what?"

"If we could start a Newcomers Club at every school. This club would be for all girls new to the school and also for those girls wanting to show them the ropes. And even during times when no new girls would enroll, this club could still meet and plan stuff that would make every girl enjoy school more. It would be a real chat room."

FYI

That's a great idea. So scout around your school and try to see if you can find a space somewhere where you and other girls interested in a real chat room could meet. Perhaps there is a large closet that's not being used or a classroom that's free at lunch. With permission, you could meet there twice a week. And the rest of the time you could Skype or chat online. Or you could just designate a table in the cafeteria and hold your informal but oh-so-helpful chats there.

> ✉ **You have one new e-mail:** Just think of all you can do or are thinking of doing to make your school less unkind. Picking on or teasing others at school or any-place else is definitely wrong and should be stopped cold. It's like a cancer that grows every day. So if it happens to you or if you observe it going on, do some-thing before it's too late. ~Lara, 13

What can help lots is to give more girl-to-girl support. And then multiply that by ten or twenty. That's exactly how much a small or mid-sized group of girls can accomplish, because cliques can be positive, not just negative. As a matter of fact, one truly good clique can overcome any number of sick ones.

A good clique is one devoted to helping girls reach their potential as individuals and as a group. Being with such a girl clique is uplifting and inspiring. It helps girls achieve their best in the classroom, on the swim team, or at the track conference meet. These girls are great chicks who will cheer and clap for each other, spurring one another on to new heights.

 NEW TEXT FROM MARTINA, 17: Always get the best that's inside you out, in track, volleyball, gymnastics, or swimming, whatever. That's how you can really overcome whomever (or whatever) tries to make you less and set an example for others.

What being with other power girls truly does is bring out and reinforce the best in all of the girls. It's like one steady candle burning on a dark night. It makes a little light, but when you add several more candles burning brightly, you have enough to get rid of the gloom and shadows. So girls doing good things for each other can start an avalanche of positive change for other girls.

Rapid Response: What You Can Do to Promote the Power of Several

1. Get together with your friends and discuss the biggest girl-world problem at your school. Some schools have more girl teasing; others have more gossiping going on. Still others have a combination of mean chick behavior face to face and behind other girls' backs, and then they really go on the attack on their fave social network. Just broach the topic with your

group and see what the upshot is where you are. Once you identify the main problem, you're that much closer to finding a solution.

2. Talk about how powerful girls can be. Know that you owe it to yourself to strive for the best you can be. Realize that it's okay to be different. Find strength in your differences and identify the special potential that your group has to bring about change.

3. Be friends with girls from various segments of your school. Power resides among the shy girls, the new girls, the girls that nobody talks to, and the girls that wear what some consider to be guy outfits or have bohemian styles or emo tendencies. Don't judge them; no matter how different, they're all girls with potential. Just how much power and talent and strength lies in each of your female classmates will emerge once you and your group befriend them, so do it.

HOW WE MADE A DIFFERENCE—A REAL-LIFE STORY FROM EMILY, 18

This is the story of a little girl back in middle school who got picked on all the time. She was overweight and wore clothes that weren't in style. There were all these preppy girls in our classes that would make fun of her to her face and behind her back, move from tables at lunch because she sat down, and spread rumors about her saying she had a nasty disease. They tormented this poor girl for years. She developed a speech problem and went to a therapy class during school and they made fun of that, too.

But she never said anything back to these girls. Not once. She always just sat there, so quiet and sweet, and just took it. Rumor after rumor was made up about her. Yet she never reacted to the bully girls, even though you could tell that it was hurting her so badly deep down inside. It must have been like a nightmare to wake up every single morning, knowing she had to face that over and over again, like she had for the longest time.

She really was the sweetest girl you could ever imagine, and I felt horrible that she got picked on so much. Two of my friends and I always tried to be kind to her and even stood up for her and sat with her when no one else would. We volunteered to be her partner in some of our classes because no one else would do it. To this day, we're still friends with this girl and have introduced her to some of the new friends we've made.

I think she has a happier life now, and I'm so glad we helped her. It's a good feeling.

Dr. Erika's Response

Congratulations to you, Emily, and to your friends, for taking this girl under your wings. Whether you realized it or not, you were exhibiting the Power of Several. It took loads of courage to stand up for her and heaps of kindness to be her partner in class. By taking that step and setting a good example, other girls will learn to follow your lead.

SMART STRATEGIES

Now let's look at some great ways to put the Power of Several into action. There's nobody more capable than an intelligent girl like you. Get together with some of your best pals or classmates and you'll be amazed by what you can accomplish. Brainstorm via e-mail, texting, or Twitter. Give status reports on the steps you're taking to reach your goal.

Smart Group Strategy #1

Aisha, 17, suggests, "Picking on other girls should have its consequences like any other bad behavior. It can lead to hurt feelings, fights, and suspension from school—and it should. But the consequences have to really be spelled out in a student handbook!"

Exactly. Have you ever closely read your student handbook? How does it handle mean chick behavior? Starting now, every school needs to spell out what unacceptable behavior is and that includes not only physical bullying but also calling names, teasing, spreading rumors, and gossiping, online or in person.

So quick, pull out the student handbook of your school. Look for the "code of conduct" section or the "school rules." Then read what it says about those mean behaviors. You'll probably find that most schools only mention physical fighting and cursing, and then give the cold shoulder to the other (and oftentimes even worse) mean behaviors. And most likely, the consequences for cyber bullying are vague. The rule will say, Don't do it! But there will be no—or hardly any—consequences mentioned.

So you and your friends can be the ones to get the message out: It's wrong to be a mean chick, and carry out a hateful trick or click. Take your girl-power group to the principal's office and voice your concerns. Ask for tougher new rules to be added to the book. It's time to start taking a stand against mean chick behavior!

Smart Group Strategy #2

Lisa Sun, 15, says, "I am pretty sure even Sasha and Malia Obama might get picked on at some time during their school years—it's that common. Wouldn't it be great if they and some other well-known young females, like Miley Cyrus or Taylor Swift, would come on TV and tell us how we can stop it so the unnecessary pain won't be passed along like some other school traditions?"

Yes, that's a great idea. With mean chick behavior so prevalent in the girl world, it would be really great to hear from some super-cool young women leaders and role models to share their stories and learn from their wisdom.

Get together with your girlfriends and make up a list of young women you admire most. Take your list to a trusted teacher or to your principal and let him or her in on your plan. Tell her you think this is an important issue—so important that the whole school should get together to learn about it. Offer to write letters to contact the speakers of your choice, to do Internet searches, whatever it takes. You never know what might come out of it. Never underestimate the power of several smart chicks like you who are determined to change the world!

Extra Credit: While you're surfing the Net looking for cool speakers to come to your school, why not hop on your school's web page? Check it out to see if there's a place or a link on the site designated for problem solving and referrals. In other words, is there a way girls can voice and vent their anger and hurt feelings and report any incidents of mean behavior and cyber bullying to a teacher, administrator, or guidance counselor that will be read at once and followed up on?

If not, get to work on it. Find out who's in charge of the web site and tell him or her what's missing. What a thrill for you and your friends to make your school's home page truly and helpfully interactive, and an accessible portal to positive change.

Smart Group Strategy #3

Terry, 14, suggests, "Get together with your friends and set up an online resource for people who have been the victims of mean chick behavior, or hand out the phone number of the guidance department, or—with permission!—the counselor's e-mail address. Or start a peer group or a teen court—any avenue you can think of, even if it means inviting powerless girls to unload on you and your friends via e-mail or instant messaging. Don't stop until the teasing stops!"

Terry has a really great idea. There is strength and safety in numbers, and by forming a help network with your friends and maybe even a trusted teacher or two, you'll be able to reach out and help those who are in pain.

Start a Facebook page that allows girls from your school to discuss the mean chick issues that bug them the most. Start a forum. Maybe you can even get the school counselor to do a weekly advice column to help address some of the larger issues. A little imagination goes a long way, so don't underestimate the power of your ideas!

FAB FIXES FOR WHATEVER ATTITUDE AILS YOU

There are times when all of us see the glass half empty instead of half full, right? Or maybe you open your closet and see nothing but tired and lame outfits and shoes that ought to take a hike—and you're not talking about your old boots!

Yeah, right, some days you wake up critical of yourself and your life, and you feel nothing you do is right, and your friends aren't so hot, either. Pretty soon, you're swimming in a sea of doubt. That's the moment you need to dig deep inside yourself and pull out your secret weapon—the best attitude that there is, and that's magnitude.

Once your magnitude comes to the forefront, nothing can stop you and your friends. Doesn't matter what's ahead—an obstacle or a decision or a way big problem, whatever. When you and your girlfriends use your magnitude to help others, you will prevail. Magnitude means—you guessed it—greatness! And greatness is your birthright. You and your group have it inside of you, so bring it out and use it.

Rx: Maximizing Your Magnitude

Always keep the following in mind:

1. Greatness is in you. Magnitude has nothing to do with brains or brawn or being big or boisterous or pretty and sweet. But it has everything to do with listening to your heart and acting your best. It means thinking of consequences before you do something. It's not rushing in, but reasoning out.

2. You have various choices. Resolve to always choose the high road, even though it might be the toughest course to success. Acting in the spirit of magnitude is reaching positively for the stars, being the most wonderful girl you can be, trying your utmost in class, at home, and in your neighborhood. It's sharing and caring and being generous and upbeat, and biting your tongue when it would've been so much fun to repeat that slur you heard, that juicy bit of gossip, because it was way funny.

3. Let it stop with you. Don't let mean chick behavior get past you any longer. Speak up and stop it— ASAP. Because now you're in the know. You know the harm that can come from being mean to another girl, so help other girls, be they the targets or the tormentors.

THE BOTTOM LINE

The bottom line about standing up to meanness among your circle of girls is the following:

- ★ Having power includes having courage, and you do, and lots of it. You've read and worked through this book because you dare to care and to be courageous.
- ★ Know that within you, you have such awesome strength that you can do just about anything you want, and then some. By banding together with other strong and independent-minded girls like you, you can multiply your girl power and accomplish more than you ever imagined.
- ★ The changes you and your girl pals instigate will begin to change the mean chicks atmosphere into a great chicks atmosphere. Cyberspace will have far fewer mean cyber chicks because of you. Yes, you are the first to spread an encouraging environment for all girls.

Conclusion

Final Words: Power Up Your Power

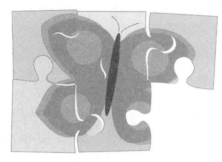

Now that you're empowered and in charge, not even the sky is the limit! You can do anything you want! By reading this book and taking action, you have provided yourself with so many new choices. Your life ahead will be one of growth, contribution, and unlimited potential, and of doing good.

Now you understand what kind of mean girl behavior can get in your way, whether it's in your face, behind your back, or worse yet, online. Now you know how to get around it or over it or how to swat it out of the way. You are able to spot, analyze, and handle any signs of mean chicks from now on. Hopefully, by reading this book and keeping up with your journal and personal blog, you've learned more about who you are each and every day and will continue to do so.

You're learning to make smart decisions and to stand up for yourself. You're not influenced by the behaviors of others. You are your own girl, you have your own style, and you rule. You are the girl of today and tomorrow, and you have the power to make change happen. There are girls all over the world who would give anything to be in your shoes, so be their heroine.

Always remember to do your best and shine as brightly as you can. You are a mega star, the radiant voice this world needs so badly. You are the youth of today and the idol of tomorrow and the day after. Be magnanimous. Be mindful and masterful. Be magnificent every moment, and be proud of the successful woman you are meant to become.

And always keep in mind that:

★ Inside every mean chick is a potentially great chick.
★ Inside every girl is the whole world.

Congratulations to you for realizing that, and best wishes!

The Chick List

Here's a great chick list to remind you of what to remember about mean chicks and about yourself as you make your way through the world with smarts and style.

Directions: Place checks next to those items you feel very confident about. Each check is worth 10 points.

_____ Can you identify the Snob at your school and not be intimidated by her?

_____ Can you spot the Gossip(s) and refuse to be drawn into her gossiping?

_____ Can you recognize the Teaser and not be bugged by her?

_____ Do you know how to handle the Bully and the Cyber Bully at your school and can you protect yourself and your friends from them?

_____ Can you bounce back after the Traitor has betrayed you without becoming bitter?

_____ Do you know where you stand in your group?

_____ Do you know what it takes to be a team player?

_____ Can you deal with the mean Clique Chicks and their harmful clicks?

_____ Do you know how to deal with Cyber Frenemies and Cyber Pit Bullies?

_____ Do you know that you alone, and you together with your friend(s), can make a difference?

Give yourself 10 points for every check!

Appendix
Cool Tools

This section offers the latest, most exciting, and best print materials plus Internet resources specifically designed to support strong and empowered girls like you:

Girls' Guides and Teen Zines

GL Girls' Life Magazine, www.girlslife.com

Seventeen Magazine, www.seventeen.com

For Fun and Further Reading

Be True to Yourself: A Daily Guide for Teenage Girls by Amanda Ford

Fab Friends and Best Buds: Real Girls on Making Forever Friends by Erika Shearin Karres

Girl Wars: 12 Strategies That Will End Female Bullying by Cheryl Dellasega

The Girl's Guide to Absolutely Everything by Melissa Kirsch

GirlWise: How to Be Confident, Capable, Cool, and in Control by Julia Devillers

Hands On! 33 More Things Every Girl Should Know: Skills for Living Your Life from 33 Extraordinary Women by Suzanne Harper, Andrea Cascardi (Editor)

Picture the Girl: Young Women Speak Their Minds by Audrey Shehyn

Respect: A Girl's Guide to Getting Respect and Dealing When Your Line Is Crossed by Courtney Macavinta

A Smart Girl's Guide to Friendship Troubles (American Girl Library Series) by Kelley Patti Crisswell, Angela Martini (Illustrator)

Super Sites

www.freshangles.com—A teen e-zine

www.cyberteens.com—A site with several areas of interest

www.gurl.com—Gurl.com has many areas of interest for teenage girls.

Yahoo.com has links to great teen e-zines. This list has pretty much something for every interest: *www.dir.yahoo.com,* and search Teenage Girls' Magazines for the most up-to-date listings.